The Naked Vet

Confessions from General Practice

John Sampson

Copyright © 2023 by John Sampson
Book Cover and Design by Paul-Hawkins.com
All rights reserved.

First edition

ISBN: 9798391111863 (Paperback)
Also available as an eBook.

No part of this book may be reproduced in any form or by any
electronic or mechanical means, including information storage and
retrieval systems, without written permission from the author, except for
the use of brief quotations in a book review.

Contents

Introduction	v
1. Vet school	1
2. The early years in practice	30
3. Romsey	62
4. Good clients, not-so-good clients	91
5. Good practices, not-so-good practices	101
6. Therapies	146
7. Nights and weekends	163
8. Bureaucracy	177
9. The end of life	205
Postscript	219
Bibliography	221
About the Author	223

Introduction

What is it like to be a vet? I've been asked that question a thousand times and there is no short answer. It depends on when you qualified, at which Vet School, whether you are in general practice - as I was - or in any of the other areas of expertise, your particular personality and your background.

Some graduates are employed by the Ministry of Agriculture (formerly MAFF and now Defra) where they become part of a large group and have the further training and support on hand. Others join industry, particularly the pharmaceutical sector, where again they learn their specialty with the help of a team and will mostly already have post-graduate degrees.

Many stay on at university, do research and become lecturers, despite the derisory salaries paid to university academics. It is true to say that a lot of them benefit from the long student vacations, but in the clinical departments which are run as full-time veterinary hospitals, the cases keep coming in whether the students are there or not. Such academics are usually of the highest standard, teaching students about the real nitty-gritty of medicine and surgery, talking them through differential diagnoses, being patient with their first fumbling attempts at surgery and sympathetically imparting knowledge to students already under huge pressure from the sheer weight of facts that they need to absorb.

In general practice, you are entering the commercial world and almost always are thrown in at the deep end. Having come out of university, on-the-job training is pretty rushed as the practicalities dictate that if you're not working there are no fees, and if there are no fees there are no salaries. Colleagues will do their best to shield and instruct you, but they are simultaneously dealing with their own cases. There is none of the 'standing around and chatting in corridors' that you may find in large organisations, nor the extended lunch breaks, early finishes or substantial paid holidays.

What all vets have in common is that when they qualify, the options are much more restricted than if you were a young doctor and the opportunities for help and guidance greatly reduced. This is chiefly because people pay directly for treatment to their animals 'at the point of delivery' whereas for humans, they don't. Veterinary practices can only afford to employ enough new graduates as their income allows, while all recently-qualified doctors have to work as house officers. They will earn exactly the same salary whether they are rushed off their feet in a huge chaotic hospital where the demands never cease, as they would working in a better-run, quieter unit where the consultants shoulder their share of the work and the young doctors can even occasionally finish their shifts on time. Many of my friends became doctors and I have the profoundest empathy for them in an age where respect for their profession is on the wane. Although I regard myself

INTRODUCTION

as a patient person, I know that I would not have made a good doctor or have been able to accept some of the worst kinds of human behaviour.

GP vets don't have to deal with time-wasters and there are no animal hypochondriacs. Few animal owners have the time or money to spare to see the vet unnecessarily (and farmers certainly can't afford it) but to judge by accounts we read from human GPs, such cases can frustratingly account for more than half their caseload. Few animals go out looking for a fight and they don't abuse their partners or offspring. They don't waste hospital workers' time in A&E, knowingly take drug overdoses, have imaginary illnesses, behave like idiots, abuse medication or injure themselves and others when drunk.

Yes, the animals that vets treat can (and do) sometimes bite, kick, scratch and peck us but somehow, they are so much more honest about it than our fellow human beings. They cannot tell us about their symptoms and that is why extensive clinical examination and lab work are so important and the basis of teaching. By the same token, they cannot confuse us with spurious or invented symptoms or downright lies. We occasionally have to deal with obnoxious owners but there are lots of sweeties out there too.

Each of the nine chapters in this book illustrates different aspects of our work and I hope I will have painted an idea of what it's like to be a GP vet in mixed practice, plus some of my own angles on animal care and health. And if you will forgive the alliteration, prepare for 'tricks of the trade', 'triumphs and 'tragedies' and plenty of 'naked truths.'

John Sampson. November 2022

Chapter 1

Vet school

'It's got a bloody sewing needle stuck in its throat!'

That was the first veterinary phrase I ever heard, and I was fifteen at the time. There were no vets among family or friends in Plymouth in those days. But my uncle and aunt were great sportspeople and had been at various times reigning champions for Plymouth and Devon in both tennis and badminton, and my aunt knew a vet through one of her clubs. She asked him if her nephew could come and 'see practice' at his Ebrington Street surgery and he agreed.

He was that kind of old-fashioned vet you don't see much today; pinstriped three-piece suit, bow tie, impeccable manners and a posh accent very much unlike most Plymothians. His practice premises more resembled a small and untidy natural history museum than the clean, clinical environments with top-of-the-range equipment that you will see in a practice today.

He was examining a cat he had admitted during that Saturday morning's surgery, not eating and unwilling to have its mouth examined. Having sedated it, he got its mouth open and there was the pointed end of the needle sticking up toward us. Neither of us could imagine what had possessed the poor cat to try and eat its owner's sewing equipment, but having anaesthetised it he managed to gently pull it out of the pharynx with its attached cotton. Fortunately, that was not too long as material like that, if it gets further down into the stomach and intestine, can bunch up and be impossible to pull out from the top. It all came out, so with an injection of an antibiotic to protect against any damage that the needle had caused, pussy woke up uneventfully and was returned to its dress-maker owner.

Three years later I was applying for vet school. In those days it was about the same as now; too many candidates applying for very few places. When I applied, the A* grade had not yet been dreamed up, but then as now, good As were essential to have any chance of getting in. This was coupled with sport and other achievements, glowing predictions and reports from your sixth form college together with any other testimonial you could obtain.

Some vet schools were notorious for only making offers to those candidates who had placed them first on the UCAS list, so you had to be careful. In Britain, without Cambridge (which had its own entrance procedure) there were five options open to me and I went for Bristol, London, Liverpool, Edinburgh and Glasgow in that order (Nottingham and Surrey have since opened new veterinary departments). The Scottish universities were so far from the west country that it was fairly impractical, but after a worrying period of silence from the others, I was offered an interview at Glasgow.

We had to find the money for our journeys up to interviews and for hotel accommodation when a return trip in a day was impossible. After a series of trains from Plymouth, I found myself the following afternoon at Glasgow University in an office with a very stern-looking panel of grey-haired senior academics in front of me. There was not a smile of encouragement from one of them as I quaked in fear, this being the first interview I had had in my eighteen years.

Their mission seemed to be to trip me up and with their increasingly difficult questions and grim faces, I began to feel distinctly uncomfortable and unwelcome. Was it because I didn't come from Lanarkshire? Do they hate the 'Sassenachs' really that much? If so, why did they drag me all the way up here, costing money mum couldn't afford? Not a glimmer of a smile or a little nod of goodwill in my direction; blimey, they take themselves seriously. They then asked me in which branch of veterinary work I might be interested. I replied 'general practice'; of that at least, I was sure. One of them, Professor Weipers, replied: 'Arrre ye aweeeerr, Mester Sampson, that Glasgoo has a greeet trrradition of rrreeeserrrch?'

I replied that I was (though what did I know?) but really felt like telling them that they were pompous old windbags and I didn't want to spend my next five years driving halfway up to the Arctic Circle learning to become a vet, even though I knew he was quite right that Glasgow was and is an excellent School. But a week later in the post came an offer; that I would be accepted if I obtained a 'Certificate of attestation of fitness'. How about that for a beautiful Scottish phrase? You could almost hear 'Laddie!' being added at the end. As far as I could tell, that certificate was equal to three passes. The conversation back in the sixth form was like this:

'Dave, you had any offers?'

'Yeah, one from Durham, two As and a B, and three Bs from Surrey.'

'Rob?'

'Still waiting for my Cambridge entrance decision. You?'

'From Glasgow. A certificate of attestation of fitness.'

Howls of derisive laughter. I had no Scottish ancestry and lived as far away from there as it is possible to be within the UK. What potential they saw in a conceited little git from Devon I don't know, but must say it was very decent of them. In the end I had an offer from Bristol, which also had a great reputation, was the nearest to home and the huge campus at Langford in the beautiful Mendip hills between Bristol and Bridgewater where you study your medicine and surgery, is indescribably picturesque.

But not everyone gets offers as easily as I did; it has become much harder. One seventeen-year-old girl, many years later, said to me in my surgery, 'I've got ten good GCSEs, I'm predicted As for A level, I've won two Duke of Edinburgh gold awards, I'm school vice-captain and skipper of hockey but I can't get a single vet school interview, what do I do?' I knew her family as they were clients and invited her to come over as an observer to the practice. She did so and promptly fainted when she saw her first operation. That in itself was not unusual as I remembered feeling 'weird' in Plymouth when I saw just a skin tumour being removed, but she persisted and returned several times. The last occasion was when she watched me do an open laparotomy where an abdomen was brimming with litres of infected serous fluid which smelt foul, with multiple metastatic cancer, and she fainted again. We had a cup of tea later and she told me that she realised the profession was not for her. Her parents came to the surgery some years later and they reported she was doing her PhD at Imperial College London, was heading for an academic career in AI and was very happy.

What was our motivation? Was it perhaps because we had been seduced by bucolic television images of James Herriot driving an ancient Ford around the beautiful Yorkshire Dales? Meeting fascinating farmers, falling in love, doing primitive small animal clinics in the living room and putting the fees into a tin on the mantlepiece? I would think back to that application process when practising in Romsey, a lovely little market town in Hampshire where I would attend careers evenings at local schools and sixth-form colleges. The sort of questions I was asked recalled my teenage years and my own motivations for becoming a vet. By that time huge numbers of young women were entering what had been a male-dominated profession and that was nothing but a good thing. Indeed, around that time the Royal Veterinary College, London announced that it had broken all records by having its first hundred per cent female entry that year. As the long queues of parents with their – nearly always – daughters edged their way towards my desk on those evenings and I heard the sort of questions they were asking, I began to think about the best ways of answering them.

The partial answer was that it did depend substantially on whether the evening was for secondary school students or sixth-form colleges. There were such embarrassingly long queues in the former all the way up to my desk that, with the permission of the Head, to gain time and reduce the wait I would gather six or seven family groups around me, do a little speech to all of them and invite questions. For the younger ones, I could not emphasise enough the importance of, quite simply, 'learning to study'. Indeed, when some announced the standard 'I want to be a vet because I love animals', I was always tempted to reply -

and sometimes did - that just about everyone loves animals one way or another and that's not a particularly good reason for wanting to become a vet. They were much better saying 'because I enjoy study', and many did.

At their stage of life, the most important factor for them was to work to their maximum capacity towards getting nine or ten GCSEs at A grades (well, maybe the odd B) because at their age, training the brain to absorb facts and recall them fast was the essential element. They may as well get used to studying just about every weekday evening because that would be what they would have to do for top A level grades and for the long years of vet school. To become sportsmen and women we need to prime and train our bodies, but our brains need also to be primed and trained to absorb and repeat countless volumes of facts. Our memories have infinite capacity but must be coaxed and taught to take vast amounts of information on board and to be able to churn them out for exam papers, whether they be GCSE geography or final year vet exams. As a teenager I foolishly imagined that our brains have some sort of limit to their capacity and could become saturated, but I soon realised that it is the opposite; the more you learn, the more you are able to learn.

For the sixth-form college students, we were able to offer more concrete advice. If they have already produced good GCSE results you take them more seriously and tell them what you can about the selection and entry process. The vet schools' admission tutors will read your A level predictions and college report, but facts speak better than guesses and those GCSE grades are a powerful argument for your selection, because if you can't get those, you will really struggle with the notoriously difficult veterinary course. Despite that, the entry competition is intense and the more you can also add to your portfolio in terms of voluntary work, awards, sports achievements and experience in leading from the front, the more the interview panel will be impressed with you. I know that these days with social media and the Internet you can get excellent CVs written for you, but never be tempted to exaggerate in them. You must have done the things that you claim on your CV because any interview panel, with suitably probing questions, will soon discover if you are not what you claim.

When you arrive up at university it may be your first time away completely alone, although if you are lucky a few of your friends may have chosen the same one. Yet sometimes it's healthy to make a complete break and start a new life. No first-year students are looking for enemies; most of them are lonely and missing their family and buddies at home too, and we all metaphorically walk around with a virtual sign hanging from our necks, 'Hello, I'm very nice, will you be my friend?' I got a university hall place at the swanky, completely new Hiatt Baker on the other side of the Downs from Bristol city centre. We were the first students in and I remember sitting on my bed amidst the lingering smells of paint, varnish and recently-unrolled flooring material and reflecting that since I didn't know a soul in Bristol, if I died that night how long would it take before someone discovered my body? Did room cleaners come in? Would the warden break in if I had locked the door? Would Mum think it weird that I hadn't rung telling her all about it?

The cleaners did come in the next morning before I went off, found me alive and they were perky as sparrows; Jean and Iris. They had that lovely burring Bristol accent.

'Right there moosh, what you studyin' then?'

'I'm going to be a vet.'
'That's good 'cos we've got this sick fish, look.'
'Yes?'
'Well, ee's got this sorta-like fungus growin' on him, look.'

I didn't know anything about fish diseases (and still don't) but I did have a little book about common ailments of domestic pets. So far that was the only veterinary book I'd possessed, as the following week when term started, we would be given the list of all our textbooks to buy. In the one I had, I turned to the goldfish section. It said that with some fungal infections if you put the fish into a strong saline solution, wait until it shows signs of discomfort and then keels over onto one side and floats to the top, and then take it out and put it back in the aquarium, you may cure it if you repeat that a few times. I told them.

'Well yeah we did that, 'cos our nan's neighbour told us that too, look.'
'And did it turn over on its side and float to the top?'
'No, it's still in there.'
'Since when?'
'Yesterday.'
'How much salt did you put in?'
'We just sprinkled a bit off our dinner, look.'

I proposed the other plan to them and said that they also might have been overfeeding it to make the water too rich, so to change that too. I don't know whether I affected my first spectacular cure that day but that fish will be dead anyway now because it was fifty years ago. I did tell them the same as I still feel, which is that although I have no real knowledge of fish diseases, they might be avoided if the poor creatures are not imprisoned in a small glass bowl with a rock or a scrap of weed for company. If people can't be bothered to buy a little aquarium to keep them healthy and stimulated, they shouldn't have fish.

Lectures were not due to begin for a week but they had told us about 'Freshers' Week' with all sorts of activities for the new arrivals, invitations to splurge our grants on memberships of this or that activity or sports club. So on the first day, I walked up to the top of the hill from the hall to take the double-decker bus the few miles into town. I sat at the middle of the top part but noticed three guys (Hiatt Baker was a men's hall like most of them in those unmixed days) who were larking around at the front and sounded quite fun. I took my courage into my hands, walked up to them and introduced myself. They became the nucleus of a group of mates in that first year and proved that if you are smiley, approachable and don't moan about stuff, up at university good things will happen to you unless you are very unlucky.

I mentioned 'grants' just now and realise that some reading this will not know what they were. In a more enlightened age when you could be educated for essential careers without crippling yourself with debt for half your life, university tuition fees were covered by the State. On top of that, most students received a 'maintenance grant' whose value was on a sliding scale depending on the income of their parents. My dad had died when I was ten and mum then got a job as a school secretary to have the same holidays as us, but her salary was low and I had the maximum grant. It was just enough (if you were careful) to pay for your hall, meals, books and expenses, though not much more. But then it was only the top five per cent who went to university at all until Tony Blair decided that fifty per cent of school leavers should go, and the rot set in. Consequently, I left university without any debts; I was lucky.

The building that housed the pre-clinical vet school at the top of Park Street was rather antiquated and had been thrown up after the Bristol bombings during the Blitz as a temporary structure for the teaching of anatomy and physiology, but they had never got round to building a new one. However, many of our lectures were just behind at the main campus and the sleek, shining new medical school. There of course, the traditional friendly rivalry between the 'medics' and the 'vets' became apparent; they accusing us of 'tramping through their nice clean med school in our filthy boots' (untrue, we wore shoes). In revenge, we mocked the first-year med students sauntering around the school with 'their stethoscopes carelessly dangling out of their pockets' playing doctors when they, like us, had barely started anatomy.

The first two years sometimes seemed far removed from what we all hoped to finally become; we spent so much time half-choking on formalin fumes in the dissecting rooms that seemed to permeate our clothes as well as our lungs. For anatomy, formalin was the only cost-effective preservative for cadavers and was used from smaller animals up to halved cattle or halved horse carcasses. It not only was acrid and unpleasant to breathe in, but it turned living tissue with its blood and vivid colours into a nasty greyish or yellowish stuff. Yet it was the only way we could learn except in occasional species which could be dissected fresh-killed. Apart from once or twice fumigating my operating theatre I haven't smelt formalin since, but if I did it would take me straight back to the anatomy dissecting rooms and the headaches you always had at the end of three hours of it.

Physiology was quite different, though we spent too much time squinting into binocular microscopes during practical histology classes (studying sectioned and stained tissue on slides). The histology lab contained about forty of them (one each) and by the time you set them up, moved backwards and forwards to find what you were looking for and asked the very patient Drs. Carter or Batten for their help, it was time-consuming.

For audio-visual lectures, the only method was presenting 'transparencies' which were slides of specimens or stained sections. From a lecturer's point of view, these were painstaking to photograph and process. They were projected onto the screen, lying right in front of powerful bulbs which could overheat and pack up. Or they actually incinerated the slides and we would occasionally watch them curling up and going brown/black right on the screen and would hear the lecturer muttering 'Damn, that was one of my best ones.'

Of course, we could not imagine that in the twenty-first century the lecturer would walk in with something that would become known as a laptop, click it onto PowerPoint and deliver lectures with five times the content we had then. The only way a teacher in those days might stimulate the students' interest as we began to drop off mid-lecture was to include a slide of a girl in a skimpy bikini or a guy with a good six-pack and then say the inevitable, 'Oh, I don't know how that one got in there.'

Nonetheless, difficult as it seemed at the time, once we started clinical work it did become obvious how important all of it had been. Many times subsequently, when facing an unfamiliar surgical intervention we would rack our brains to take us back to our anatomy lectures to remember where that artery or nerve was to avoid sectioning it. Or which muscle lies over which, in order to get at something.

. . .

Tough as it was, the great thing about the vet course was that it got more and more interesting as the years advanced and the third year arrived with fascinating subjects like pharmacology, virology, bacteriology, mycology, parasitology and immunology. There weren't many ribald or tasteless comments from lecturers in those days as it was enough to impart all that information in just five or six years, but two stick in my mind. Genetics, embryology, infertility, artificial insemination, gynaecology and obstetrics in LA (large animal) practice were hugely important in those days and in the fourth year we had six lecturers dedicated purely to those subjects. During a practical, one of the girl students asked, 'Dr. Vicars, how is this equine obstetrical speculum used?' 'Bend over and I'll show you,' he joked, as ever with the unlit pipe permanently clamped between his teeth.

Try saying that these days. Of the thirty-seven of us in our year, nine were girls. And they were tough cookies, so any sexist banter from us was immediately countered by wit and humour from them, rather than taking offence. Political correctness and the right to be offended by everything had not yet been invented by university sociology departments, and before the important phrase, 'objectivising women' had been dreamed up, too, as in one practical class where we were doing live anatomy with a very well-behaved mare. We had all had a go at feeling around her stifle joint (the knee, basically, but in horses it's situated right up near the groin) and someone commented on how quiet the mare was being. The lecturer replied, 'Well if she was feeling my inner thigh like that, I think I'd stand rather quietly too.' I've just told my nineteen-year-old daughter that one as I type it and she replied that she is shocked; unreconstructed times, I suppose, but I think they were more fun.

The army of lecturers we had for the LA (large animal) areas mentioned above contrasts sharply with the few that taught us small animal (SA) medicine and surgery, and Dr. John Yeats had to cover principles of surgery as well as general, ophthalmic and orthopaedic. It was he who pointed out to us that surgical masks are not much use unless you change them every ten minutes or so. After that sort of time, they become saturated with the surgeon's breath and any cough, sneeze or even intemperate shout could result in an aerosol of mouth organisms over the case being operated on.

To an extent, he said, the same applied to surgical gloves, which, although sterile at the outset, are very flimsy and easily damaged. If you rip one, you change it but it's easy to overlook one being slightly punctured by a suture needle or a sharp piece of bone and, with hands getting hot and sweaty, out would jet millions of bacteria from the pores, however thoroughly you've scrubbed up. As mixed GPs we had to take particular precautions because it was common that you came back from LA jobs on farms pretty messy and then had to do an emergency SA operation that was waiting for you at the surgery. Even if you washed and scrubbed your hands raw, there was still the danger that residues of the dirt and greasy coats that had permeated your skin and got under your fingernails, were still there. I have to admit that I often knew that I shouldn't have been doing certain SA operations in those conditions, but when you're single-handed, you have no choice.

At Bristol a memorable piece of university fooling around once a year was Rag Week. I don't think they do them anymore now but they were a hoot; a whole week of silliness, stunts, drinking and raising money for Bristol charities. All the sports and general clubs contributed something; we were surrounded by collection tins being shaken, were happy to put some of our grants into them for a good cause and it was all very light-hearted. Bristol is mostly on a long slope from the leafy Downs at the top until you get right down to the bottom; the docks and the Avon. The dock area of town is now completely rebuilt and full of pubs, clubs and leisure activities but was a bit grim in those days and students didn't often go down there.

The main university buildings were on a flat section in the middle, after the steep Whiteladies Road and before dropping via the equally steep Park Street to the bottom. One year for Rag the mountaineering club organised a full-on attempt from their 'base camp' by the Council offices up to the 'summit' (the university Wills building), scaling the treacherous north face of Park Street. They worked in stages all the way up the hill with a second base camp in the middle (there was a cider barrel inside, I was told) in full kit; all the ropes, crampons, picks, wedges and oxygen masks for the final assault on the peak, calls of 'pulley coming down on green' until they made the top.

Talking of unreconstructed times, one of the decorated lorries in the inevitable Rag procession on the final Saturday through Bristol was the 'Rag Queen' float. I suppose it would be anathema now, but it was with the background of regularly televised 'Miss Great Britain' or 'Miss World' contests which seemed harmless enough and were then not at all frowned upon.

The contest for Rag Queen (who, unlike in many beauty contests, was clever as well as beautiful) took place the week before. All the faculties entered their own contestant; the ballroom above the Long Bar at the Students' Union was booked for the evening and it was quite a spectacle. Students clutching their pints lurched up the stairs and for a modest entrance fee that also went to the charities, arrived in their droves for the show. Each girl was to be introduced by an 'MC' (one of the students from her department) wearing a dinner jacket and she was then interviewed by him. No swimming costumes for the girls, just a long dress or ball gown and they all tried to make it as funny as possible.

In our fourth year, a few of us decided to enter a vet school candidate and I had persuaded one of the stockmen at Langford to drive the twenty-six-mile return journey in a van to help us out, bless him. Our candidate was named Clara Butt, and when it was our turn I was passed the microphone as her MC. A spotlight came on over a door at the side, and our 'girl' was led in, in a head collar accompanied by one of the vet students wearing a lab coat. She was a beautiful white Saanen goat. She brought the house down and I woffled about her as best as I could but I don't think they heard much of my commentary over the laughter. I tried to get them to hear '... *she's had considerable experience in most fields ...*' and other inanities but soon it was over and Patrick led her off.

The voting took place over the next few days and she came THIRD. The Rag Queen was traditionally accompanied in the Saturday procession by her 'attendants'- the two runners-up - and Clara should technically have been on the float but she became indisposed, so we withdrew her. The number four contestant took her place and pluckily announced that she was happy to have been beaten by a goat. It was all very silly.

The other big event of Rag Week was the evening four-hour human-powered go-cart race at a nearby stadium. It was nearly always won by the engineers of course; everyone had to build their own carts from scratch using scrap materials, so bicycle pedals, gears and chains, pram wheels and a chassis made out of anything available to produce the most eclectic mixture of mad machines. Each driver then pedalled like hell for ten minutes before changing over. I heard that the cart became part of the curriculum in the engineering departments, but the fitness freaks from the sports clubs put in a good show too. The stadium was always packed, tins being shaken all over the place and Bristol City Council always warmly thanked the students for their time, effort and money (though the academic staff may not have been so happy with all the missed lectures).

We had quite a lot of those in the big lecture theatre at the med school, with the student entrances at the back and the front doors purely for the use of teachers. We were having a lecture for vets, medics and dentists on coagulation of the blood when we heard a bicycle bell outside the lecturers' entrance. As a Rag stunt (they were pretty inevitable) a student opened the door, walked in, rang his bell again, carefully propped his bike up against the lecturer's podium, and went and sat down. The academic didn't blink. 'There, ladies and gentlemen, is another example of how clots can travel.' He got more applause than the student.

The clinical work was all done at the huge veterinary hospital at Langford, out in lovely countryside thirteen miles west of Bristol. In the early years we had a number of coach trips out there for lectures or early introductions to clinical work and it was fascinating to see the 'big boys and girls' of the fourth and fifth years about their lectures and clinic rotations. I write 'and girls', but in those days, as I have mentioned, vet students were mostly men. This was partly due to the pre-eminence of farm practice, though it was disappearing. It was physically tough going and though many women were – and still are - up to the task, most vets now think that spending the day in a nice warm surgery in the middle of winter is more fun than getting cold, wet and trampled-on outside.

The fact of the profession currently becoming dominated by women leads me to mention the 'Dr.', 'Mr.', 'Miss' and 'Mrs.' situation, as there were certain conventions in Britain that have recently been overhauled. The medics who qualified as 'doctors' did not actually have the letter 'D' for 'Dr.' in their degrees. At Bristol they gained the degrees MB, ChB (Bachelor of medicine, Bachelor of surgery) and the vets' degree was BVSc. (Bachelor of veterinary science). Only those who had taken PhDs or other academic doctorates were technically permitted to style themselves 'Dr.', but newly qualified medics did so as a courtesy title because of the distinction between a physician and a surgeon. Physicians were called 'Dr.' and surgeons 'Mr.' (if men, whether human, veterinary or dental) and to most extents, the tradition remains in the case of senior surgical registrars or consultant surgeons who, having first been called 'Dr.', once they pass their Fellowship exams, prefer to re-adopt the title 'Mr.'

But this does not take women into account and with so many more of them becoming vets, they found themselves being 'Miss' or 'Mrs.' which could be taken by the general public to suggest a less qualified status. And within the last thirty years when Britain had been flooded with graduates from veterinary schools in Europe and the world (most of whom have that letter 'D' in their qualifications), the system became unbalanced. On the plate outside veterinary practices, you could now have 'Dr. Patel', 'Dr. Schmitt' or 'Dr. Assiz' for the foreign graduates and then 'Miss Smith' or 'Mrs. Jones' for the British-trained ones. And so, for graduates of what is regarded by many as the best surgical and clinical training in the world, the opinion of the public was often that they may be inferior to the others. Receptionists everywhere got fed up with being asked 'Is Dr. Hernandez a better vet than Miss Jackson?' Finally, the misunderstanding was addressed by notifying all vets that they could adopt the same courtesy title as the medics if they chose to. Many have taken that option and others still do not, preferring the old system.

Having shared houses and flats in the middle years, when we arrived at Langford we were all reluctantly obliged to go back into hall as we needed to be on the spot at night when interesting cases had been admitted and were being dealt with by the full-time clinicians. But at least we could go for great country walks and did have a rugby and cricket pitch, plus a squash court to help us retain our sanity. One Saturday, mum had come up to visit when Alan Vinnecombe, my next-door-room neighbour walked into mine without knocking, having just played squash and was clutching around his waist a very small towel.

'John, can I borrow your shamp... oh, sorry... I didn't know you had company.'

'Alan, my mum; mum, Alan.'

'Hello Mrs. Sampson, sorry again, can I take the shampoo?'

'Sure.'

'Bye-bye Mrs. Sampson.' To which mum replied,

'Nice to have seen so much of you!'

The Langford complex having originally been a 'stately home' and then enlarged with new building to become a campus, some of the original features of a classical estate remained. One was a 'ha ha'; a wall between two levels of grazing land which avoided fencing and involved a drop of maybe two metres. Below that we annually played the 'ha ha' game, an improvised form of pseudo-rugby where the ball was filled with sand and impossible to kick or move very far. If it hadn't rained, the mini-pitch was hosed down before the match and became so messy that by halfway through, they were all covered in thick mud from boots up to - and including - face and hair.

We also had an annual staff/student normal rugby match which the students usually won, and a cricket match. In the final year the staff were captained by lecturer Jim Pinsent, head of the PTU (Practice Teaching Unit) and a very fine clinician. At the warm-up, as wicket-keeper he was taking balls fired at him very hard from close range quite effortlessly and hardly noticing them. It turned out that when he was a student at the Royal Veterinary College, London he had been a reserve keeper for Middlesex County Cricket Club. We lost.

Having been a runner all the way through school, with athletics in the summer and cross-country in the winter, I had no idea about rugby. One afternoon after lectures, I was jogging back from a five-miler and was stopped by Howie Thresher, the skipper of the vet students XV.

'John, you can run, can't you?'
'Derr…'
'Can you run the wing for us on Saturday?'
'Do you mean rugby?'
'Yeah.'
'But I don't know the rules.'
'No problem, you'll be out on the left wing and you just run for the line.'
'Where is it, here?'
'No, it's away at Blagdon.'

Sounded straightforward enough, except that I'd never played and realised that he must have been pretty desperate to have invited the rugby equivalent of a number eleven batsman who can't bowl. Besides, I'd heard of the Blagdon squad. When we arrived for the fixture, they seemed to have come to resemble the large tractors they drove. There wasn't much employment over there except in farming and they looked as if they could carry 40kg grain sacks on each shoulder.

'But Howie, I can't play against them, they look like the kinfolk of Grendel.'

'Oh, they're completely unfit, look at those cider-bellies, you'll outrun them easily.'

Maybe so, but I was used to running fast in a straight line and knew nothing of dummies, swerves or overlaps. And although I had powerful legs, I had a skinny torso and weighed under nine stone so each time I was body-checked by one of them it felt as if I'd run at full speed into a tree. Play had to be extended for an hour's injury time (mine), but afterwards we all had a laugh about it over a pint in the clubhouse when I got back from intensive care.

The final years always put on a pantomime just before the Christmas vacation. Ours was called 'Pus in boots' (not 'Puss') and the year before, the finalists had put on 'Porky and the Bungle Book', named after one of the few unlamented lecturers, who was awful and did not last long. He taught pig medicine and was known as 'porky' after his subject and his girth. The pantos were mostly about Langford, the students and the staff of course, although we did present in one sketch a little comic opera. There, an old lady's two cage birds (a green one and a red one) had escaped and flown to the top of a high tree. No one would rescue them except Tom the village simpleton, who climbs up a tall ladder and retrieves only the red one. When back on the ground he sings to the old lady that he didn't bring the green one down because it 'Isn't ripe yet'. Our opening number and finale were 'There's no business like vet business', adapted from Irving Berlin's song from 'Annie get your gun', with such lines as,

> *Everything about it is appealing,*
> *Anything the client will allow,*
> *Nowhere can you get that happy feeling,*
> *When you're palpating a pregnant cow.*

And it ended with,

> *Even when they tell you that you won't go far,*
> *But soon you qualify and there you are.*
> *Now at least you're going to get a decent car,*
> *So that's the end of the show.*

Although those last two years were solid medicine and surgery, I don't remember anyone ever discussing the basic differences between them; they were studied as different subjects and just 'were'. Yet they are completely different entities and in every respect the opposite of each other. Successful surgeons and successful physicians are an entirely contrasting species; it takes a certain character and personality to shine in one, yet the opposite in the other and few become totally successful in both.

Surgeons need to be quick and decisive, while physicians need to give their patients time. Successful physicians need patience and empathy while most surgeons wouldn't know what they are. Surgeons need courage, physicians need reflection and critical judgement. There is everything in medicine that is intuitive: time to listen to the patient or owner and examine the case thoroughly, to keep all options open from the beginning, to work out in one's head the list of clinical possibilities, choose the most likely diagnosis and treat accordingly.

Conversely, there is nothing in the slightest bit intuitive about sticking a scalpel deep into living, breathing tissue and being faced with blood, fat, serum, other bodily fluids, pus or intestines pouring out. It goes against every grain of rational human behaviour and it is true that because it's unnatural, all junior surgeons at the beginning are nervous and clumsy. It also explains why they must be minutely supervised whereas young physicians can get on with their jobs mostly on their own. Surgeons are a grown-up version of the boys that used to spend their time at skateparks performing terrific antics, showing off in front of their mates and doing their best to brain themselves. Physicians are more gentle, more relaxed and prefer games where tactics, brainpower and intelligence are superior to exhibitionism and brute strength.

In my practising time I think it was true to say that men were happier with operating though this was not a rule. Equally, if I overheard a woman vet consulting, I often thought how much better she was at it than I. But options are nowadays rather more open, although women who want to train as surgeons still have the blight of sexism to contend with. She will then be admitted to their private rugby club if she has the patience to tolerate them as colleagues.

As an example of that, I was much later employed purely as a 'cutter' at a big practice in Salisbury for a couple of weeks. A pleasant (but rather twittery) recent graduate came into the theatre where I was doing an aural resection. That was a cosmetic op on the ears of dogs who have chronic infections and which takes about an hour per side; and as long as that principally because of the number of stitches you put in and the necessity to place them at just the right angles. She said:

'John, I've got an appointment at a quarter to three, do you think I've got time to do a cat spay?'

'Well, it's two o'clock; yes, you've got plenty of time.'

'But what about my 2.45 appointment?'

'You'll be fine; it'll only take you twenty minutes.'

'But what if it takes longer?'

'If you get stuck, I'll help you out.'

Half an hour later: 'John I can't find the ovaries and I've got that 2.45 appointment.'

'Pull on the proximal left horn of the uterus, the ovary should come up to the incision.'

'Thanks.'

A short time later…

'I haven't found the uterus, either.'

At that point, I left what I was doing, re-scrubbed, told her to go to her appointment, finished off the cat spay and then the resection. She came back into the theatre.

'John, could you have look at my 2.45 case? It's a mammary growth and I don't know whether it needs operating on.' I am pretty patient but she was beginning to get on my nerves. I saw the case with the owner present, took her outside (I thought) out of the hearing of the client and said, 'You really are being stupid about this. All mammary tumours must be removed quickly as a percentage of them are malignant and any delay can result in their spreading through the body.'

She later told me, rather pathetically, that the client had overheard the conversation and thought that I had been needlessly aggressive towards her. Do you see? Arrogant surgeons? I am told that in the human field most house officers are glad if their surgical consultants even know their names after six months of traipsing behind them. And young vets do need a bollocking from time to time; it helps to build character as I discovered in Wokingham, as I will explain.

As further proof of the courage and skill of professional surgeons, when I was much later working in the French Antilles I got to know an anaesthetist who was employed at the General Hospital in the capital, Fort-de-France. She invited me to dinner and offered to let me spend a day in the theatres there. I took a day off and that one happened to be the spinal orthopaedic day, with three theatres, each with two tables, running simultaneously. The atmosphere was unlike anything I had ever experienced. At home operating was fairly quiet, with perhaps a bit of chatting during the less tricky, routine ops. But there it was booming; those huge, jovial black surgeons doing unbelievable interventions and shouting and joking with each other all the way through. One was correcting scoliosis in a young guy where there was terrifying distortion but he attacked it with extraordinary bravado. And all the time nattering away to his colleague on the opposite table who was busy decompressing three adjacent prolapsed discs via a dorsal approach, gaily rongeuring off the dorsal spines to get at the cord.

I glanced over at the face of that intubated patient and recognised him. An hour earlier a nurse had come in and asked if anyone spoke Spanish, as a patient from a neighbouring island who was awaiting surgery didn't speak French and was very frightened. I had gone and chatted to him and then half an hour later he was under anaesthetic and being operated on. The surgeon shouted, '*John, viens voir*' and he had the spinal cord held in his retractor slightly out of the canal. But as he looked over to me, I saw it stretching away from where it should be (I really didn't know they were that extensible) and I shouted 'Faites attention!' as he looked back to watch what he was doing. And in another theatre, a surgeon was operating with the same abandon on a horrific back injury following a riding accident. I admired their courage.

Langford was all study and not much else, but there were lighter moments. The Langford Arms was a short walk from our hall and a crowd of us after too much to drink around 11.30 pm one Friday broke into an egg-production unit at a farm close to the pub. There being no one around, we decided to form the 'Ad Hoc Battery Hen Liberation Army'.

So on a number of subsequent Saturday evenings, we were selling a couple of 'fresh prime chickens' down at the Long Bar at the Students Union in Bristol. Many of the students, particularly the humanities ones, seemed to have spent their entire grant by half term and were so hungry that they would buy anything cheap. We plucked and gutted them (the chickens that is) in the showers at the hall until the warden discovered the blood and feathers and put an end to it but one must have been overlooked.

The following Saturday, a student came up to us and said, 'You sold me what you called a prime young bird last week but we took it out of the oven and there was a hard-boiled egg inside, so it was a scrawny old layer, wasn't it?' To which, thinking on our feet, we replied 'Well lucky you, you got this week's free egg!'

Lock-ins were frequent and even encouraged by James, the landlord, to sell more beer. He was a tall, handsome and well-spoken guy and we imagined he might have been a Second World War fighter ace, though the truth was probably more prosaic. His standard response to whatever you ordered - even just half of bitter - was 'A very wise choice, if I may say so.' At one lock-in when he had remembered to bolt the door, there was a hammering, all the glasses went behind the bar and he admitted the policeman, with, 'Welcome to the AGM of the Langford cricket club, officer. We were just discussing who would be opening bat.'

The next time we were not so lucky. Someone must have left; the door was unlocked and a motorcycle cop strolled in. Removing his gloves and saying nothing, he filed past us all very slowly, looking down at our illegal drinks and each of our faces in turn. We thought we're in for it now, and there's Jim's licence too, complaints to Professor Grunsell, maybe proceedings. He took off his helmet and then went up to the bar with 'Got any cigars, Jim?' He bought them, had another look at us, replaced his helmet and walked out. But he'd made his point and we didn't do it again.

Those final Langford years were packed and exhausting. You are nearly there, lectures all morning and all afternoon diagnosing, treating animals and operating on them, all of those under supervision. Although in theory in the finals you can be asked about anything you have learned in those five or six years, they are mostly about surgery, medicine or public health although occasionally questions about jurisprudence (the laws applying to animals) may creep in. I had failed the clinical pathology papers in the fourth year and had to go back at the beginning of September to re-sit them over two days of exams, but had gone over to Denmark to revise. This came about in a curious way.

Through the last four years of the course, we all had to 'see practice' during the holidays. We were each allotted a 'foster practice' to which we went back regularly and also some specialist practices (SA, farm, equine, poultry) to which we went just once. My foster practice was in Cheltenham (the flamboyant and erudite Tim Eaton's practice) and they were excellent teachers. My specialist equine practice was in Wickham, Hampshire, which was a large mixed practice and I was assigned either to horse vets Charles Roberts or John Fowler. They were both good clinicians and taught me a huge amount (though I must admit I prefer the memory of riotous parties with the nurses). John was married to a beautiful Danish girl, Dorthe, and one evening just after getting my 'failed' result they had invited me to dinner. I told them that I didn't have much money but was looking for somewhere to revise where I could also keep physically fit. Dorthe mentioned that her nearly-retired parents in Denmark had a holiday home on Fano, near Esbjerg in Jutland, that was right by the beach and they would be there for the whole summer holiday. If I liked she would ring them and ask if I might stay. They apparently had a very lively Pointer, Luuker, and she said that as my end of the bargain I could keep him exercised.

They agreed and I drove up through France, Belgium and Germany in my old and badly overheating Austin A30, sleeping in the car. It was as well that I took it as just the textbooks I had with me would have mostly filled a rucksack and no room for my clothes and guitar. I arrived in the centre of Esbjerg as agreed where they would meet me, but somewhere in those intervening countries I had lost the piece of paper containing their address. I tried ringing Dorthe in the UK from a phone box having worked out how to use Danish kroner coins, but she was out so I went to the main police station. I knew Dorthe had been called Tranberg before marrying John, so I tried to explain to the policeman.

'Can you help me? I am looking for a Mr. Tranberg.'

'Tranberg is the most common family name in Esbjerg,' the officer laughed.

'Oh, I remember, his first name is "Grosserer", his name is Herr Grosserer Tranberg.'

'That means "wholesaler".' It was true; in Denmark they didn't use given names much and you were usually referred to as the name of your job. Even if you worked gutting herrings, you would be known as 'Herr herring-gutter Larsen', they later explained to me. Finally, I remembered that Dorthe had mentioned that her father owned a big shop selling bicycles.

'Yes, I know who that is, I'll ring him for you,' chuckled the officer. Full marks to him for his English, I thought. Ouve came over and collected me and I spent the first night in their huge apartment in Esbjerg. They were the sweetest old couple and I was introduced to Luuker who was fascinated with me and clearly lacked exercise.

The next morning I followed their car to the summer house, which was big and indeed right on the beach. I spent the next six weeks trying to learn the difference between squame cell carcinomas, astroctytomas and haemangiomas on the beach with Luuker by my side, or we ran and swam. The three of us ate together, I didn't see any other person for that period and didn't want to. They were so funny and such good company that even if they occasionally said to me 'You're a young man, you'll be getting bored with us old people, why don't you go out for the evening?' I always assured them that I was perfectly content with their company. I did relent one evening, though, when they insisted once again and I jogged a mile or so to a bar where they said there would be young people. There were quite a few students there but they were having fun together and took no notice of me (why should they?) and I walked home.

The last week, however, they announced that friends were coming to dinner with their eighteen-year-old daughter. I was as usual on the beach with Luuker, my books and guitar, and a girl appeared. And rather stunning she appeared, too. Apparently, they had arrived a bit earlier and had told her to walk along the beach to find me. Anna had come back to the house saying that there's almost nobody left down there but a black boy, is that him? I wasn't quite black but after six weeks on the beach, you can imagine.

I passed the re-sit in September and enjoyed the final year so much that it swept by. And I was back in Denmark immediately after the final exams. Mum rang to say I was now a vet and told me the date of the graduation ceremony. I was having so much fun up there with Anna and her family that I at first told mum that I wasn't coming back for graduation, but she very sharply told me that I WAS coming back and she had waited a LONG TIME for that moment. Ah well, ok mum ... and in fact you did have to be present, as it is then that you are awarded your MRCVS and you swear the veterinary form of the Hippocratic oath. All good things had to come to an end, but they were to lead to much better.

Chapter 2

The early years in practice

For my first job I wanted a practice specialising in what we call 'large animals' (LA), that is, horses and farm animals (though it would extend to elephants and all the rest). This was my main interest and, as I've described, we were very well trained in that kind of work. If possible I wanted to work in the west country, and the first interview was at a slightly archaic LA practice in Camborne, Cornwall, but they could only offer me £2000 a year, in 1971. This did include free accommodation and a car but even then, I thought it was not a sum I could really live on.

Then in the *Veterinary Record*, which is the main organ for job notices, I saw a temporary assistantship in Woking, Surrey for six months. Small animals only, but I guessed that it might be worth getting some experience in that before looking later for a mixed practice further southwest. I was replacing the boss, who was having heart surgery and I gained great experience from Keith Linington, Tony Wilson-Jones and John Wicks.

It was my first job, and the clients must have been a bit baffled sometimes when I suddenly made up an excuse, such as an urgent phone call, to nip into another consulting room to ask one of them for advice. For example, we had covered testicular tumours in pathology but I had no idea about a condition where some small irritation starts dogs licking their scrotum and then they make it worse and worse until it is livid red and oozing serum. I had not a clue what to call it or how to treat it, and went in to ask John.

'Scrot rot,' he said, 'Give it an injection of propen/dexamethasone and give the owners Tetradelta ointment.'

'Thanks, John. I owe you a pint. How many tubes of Tetradelta?'

'One... is it a big dog?... oh, then make it three.'

Scrot rot? I wasn't going to find that in a medicine textbook. So for the sake of the client, I invented on the spot the term 'scrotal dermatitits' which I suppose was probably what it was, treated it and got on with the next one. Such dogs are also frequently hyper-sexed and the action is almost always a result of frustration, so neutering can be the more permanent answer.

It was - and still is - a big question in practice; to neuter or not to neuter? In the male it's called castration and in the female we usually use the term spaying. And vets around the world will be discussing this with SA clients today. The answer varies between the species and the sexes. Animal owners who are men will say to us, 'I wouldn't want that done to me, would I? It's not natural' and women may say, 'But it is natural for a bitch (a female dog) or a queen (the general term for a female cat) to have little ones, isn't it?' And of course they are right, but only to an extent; the crucial factor being the interpretation of the word 'natural'. Our domestic animals are our friends as well as our responsibility; they form an integral part of our lives and our homes and when they die it's almost as much of a tragedy as the death of a human loved one.

But could you call theirs a 'natural' life? Certainly, for most domestic pets it's a pleasant one, with food supplied, strokes and cuddles, regular exercise, baths and shampoos, flea treatment, worming, trips to the vet when unwell and a nice warm basket. But is this natural? Well in one way it is, in the sense that it has become the accepted norm since animals were first domesticated, in modern homes. But in another sense, it's far from natural feral conditions. Nature can be kind and she can be cruel, but domestication takes our pet animals out of nature and into our hands.

As far as breeding is concerned, it is we as owners who make the decisions. Do we want our new male kitten to grow up as a tomcat, yowling to get out, finding females where he can and having a revoltingly smelly wee, or do we want a friend and companion? The same applies to female kittens. It may be 'natural' for them to become pregnant on their first heat at seven or eight months so long as there is a tom about, but do we really want her to have kittens when she is that young herself? Nature demands it, but wouldn't we rather have her purring on our lap and catching mice?

For male dogs, many 'entire' (that is to say, uncastrated) ones are no trouble at all and you would hardly know that there is a healthy amount of testosterone rushing around in their veins, but others show acute signs of frustration and either try to escape or attempt to wrap themselves around your leg in a loving embrace. As for bitches, having pups is a very 'natural' thing to do; some owners do go for that option, and for breeders it is their expertise and their livelihood. It varies so much from family to family; some want the experience of having their bitch mated, living through the pregnancy with her and hoping that she will be able to give birth without veterinary assistance. But things can go wrong, and there the 'natural' becomes the 'assisted'. Then it's the car to the vet's; maybe Oxytocin injections when things are very slow, maybe internal intervention or where all else fails, caesarien section.

After whelping (having the pups), post-operative infection may intervene; the pups may have been born weak, she may not take to them or reject them entirely. She may not lactate (produce milk) in the quantities necessary; the pups may have difficulty in latching on to very small nipples and there are other gynaecological conditions that can need veterinary treatment. It's time-consuming and it can be costly; some owners have that sort of time and money available and some do not. It is a clear choice and one that all owners of female animals must make. Generally speaking, if we take on a female puppy, most of us decide that we just want 'her', to love, to walk, to feed, to enjoy and to become part of the family, rather than a breeding machine.

So, to the men who tell us that they would 'never want it to happen to them', that is a perfectly acceptable comment, except that they are free to have a sex life; while physically preventing an entire male dog from going out and doing what is most natural to him seems unfair, if not actually cruel. And an un-spayed bitch comes 'on heat' about every six months; she is ovulating, she is producing large quantities of the sex hormone oestrogen and she feels she wants to mate. So again, stopping her from doing what nature intended by keeping her away from prospective partners seems unfair too. I hope this summarises my view of the 'breeding or not breeding' debate, though it's my own and doesn't necessarily reflect the view of the whole profession.

I have mentioned gynaecological conditions, and there

is one which is very important and owners of un-spayed bitches do need to know about. This is a serious condition called 'pyelometritis' or 'pyometra' for short. It is most common in 'maiden' bitches (those that have never had pups) when they reach, maybe, seven or eight years old, or less commonly in those who had a litter or two when young and never bred again. The owners will have noticed, in the previous heats (periods of sexual activity), that they have become irregular; that she loses more blood than usual and maybe a slightly purulent (pus-like) discharge. She may be listless and off colour as well, but then it may temporarily improve until the next heat. What is happening is that a slow and (at first) sterile infection is building up in the uterus (the womb) but it only happens during the heat or soon after. On the next one, the disease then flares up into a life-threatening condition. She becomes very unwell indeed, goes off her food, drinks excessively, her abdomen may be tense and her vulva becomes clearly swollen even though the heat is over.

The worst cases are the so-called 'closed' pyometras where the cervix remains completely shut and no discharge is seen. In these, the uterus is going a nasty shade of purple and is filling up with infected pus. The 'open' cases are less acute as at least some of the poisonous material is escaping; the owners see it and are faster to bring her to the surgery. In either case she must be operated on immediately and not even left until the next morning as she will get worse very quickly and perhaps not even withstand the anaesthetic. I cannot count the times that I operated on these in the middle of the afternoon between clinics or right after evening surgery. They are very toxic and you have to be careful not to anaesthetise too deeply; just enough to be unconscious but no more.

We remove an infected uterus up to twenty times its

normal size and filled with foul-smelling material and so long as it has not ruptured, spilling its contents into the abdomen, the prognosis is good. Alas, there are neglected cases where rupture has occurred and then you are faced with septic peritonitis through the abdomen, which is a different matter. Sometimes the uterus is so massive that it almost fills the whole abdomen, so the intravenous fluid therapy during surgery has to be increased drastically at the point where the uterus is removed as that action is accompanied by a dramatic fall in blood pressure and surgical shock.

Nevertheless, the happy outcome for most cases is that once that huge, toxic thing is removed, they recover very quickly and the ones who were admitted close to death can be jumping up and down in their kennels soon after. Owners often used to say when bringing her back to have the stitches out, 'It was so slow that we didn't really notice her deterioration, but she hasn't been as well as this for years.'

There is a downside to neutering, though, and no intervention of that nature can be without some side effects. This is the possible tendency to put on weight. However, plenty of neutered animals get tubby while others remain slim and the truth is that often it's more a question of diet than neutering. When clients asked me about it, my reply was always that I see a lot of overweight neutered animals and a certain number of un-neutered ones too and in either case they don't gain weight from 'breathing the air'. Overweight and then overt obesity are a fact of life in our modern world and exactly the same diet and exercise rules apply as they do to our own species. We may flop at home and gorge on pizzas; dogs may sit in their baskets and worry us for snacks and the result will be the same. Regular exercise is as important for them as it is for us as well as a sensible diet with balanced levels of proteins, fats, fibre, carbohydrates, vitamins and minerals. Human beings are free to 'dig their own graves with their teeth' but it's us animal owners who decide how to feed our pets for optimum health.

With all routine operations such as neutering there is a tiny risk of unexpected death during surgery, though modern anaesthetics are very safe compared with the old methods such as chloroform. For dogs, induction (that is, the first big intravenous dose to produce immediate unconsciousness) was then and still often is by thiopentone, but as one of our anaesthetics lecturers, Dr. Lucke, pointed out, 'It's fatally easy to administer' and being given rapidly, the dose must be minutely calculated. Thiopentone is excellent but short-acting and the next step is intubation (putting an endotracheal tube down into the windpipe or 'trachea') and using one of several gases to maintain unconsciousness for the length of the intervention. Cats are rather different as they have a very narrow larynx (the entrance to the trachea) which often goes into spasm when touched by an endotracheal tube so they are trickier to intubate. But some excellent medium and long-term intravenous anaesthetics have been developed for them – in my time principally one called Saffan – that are very safe and can be 'topped-up' through the operation.

Losing an old and sick animal during anaesthesia is to be expected occasionally but I only lost one young, apparently fit animal in a routine operation, and that was indeed a cat. I had induced her with Saffan as usual and was halfway through a routine spaying when suddenly her respiration and heart stopped. No attempts at resuscitation were successful and I had to break it to the owner on the phone, feeling very embarrassed and inadequate. I asked whether she had noticed anything strange about the six-month-old kitten.

'Well, yes, actually, we noticed that she sometimes would keel over and lie on her side as if she had fainted, and then slowly get up again. I forgot to mention it this morning when I dropped her off; do you think it was connected?'

'Yes, I should think so. It sounds as if she had a heart defect. I always listen to the heart before sedation as a routine but you can't always hear something.'

'Well, in that case it's not your fault.'

'Thank you for being so understanding, and again I am sorry.' But when these things happen you feel rotten.

I digressed, but let me go back to my first practice in Woking. The three permanent vets were invaluable to me in those 'apprenticeship' months where I was trying to build all the thousands of lectures and the textbooks into the realities of life in general practice. They were very patient with me in 'post-Langford' surgery, talking me through even the simplest interventions, and as I wrote in the previous chapter, it is always a slow process. Some vets get the hang of it and others remain much better doing clinics and leaving the messy work to the cutters.

I had been given lodgings paid for by the practice with a nice old lady living on Horsell Common outside Woking who seemed to need the company as much as the money. Kind as she was, I couldn't help ruefully reflecting during the evenings that sitting in my room or watching TV with her was not what most single twenty-five-year-olds expect on their first job. But Keith came to the rescue when a place in the rented house he was sharing became vacant and I moved in there. There were four of us and we shared the cooking rota but I was rubbish and one lunchtime had shot back to quickly prepare a stew for the evening, as it was my turn and I knew I'd be finishing last. It really didn't seem to be thickening so I added some more lentils which didn't change anything so I threw the rest of the packet in and left the liquid to stew without heat as I shot back to the practice. When I got in that evening, Keith and Tim were mirthfully shouting, 'We've cut out your piece for you.'

Those six months were very useful and now I saw an LA job in Wokingham, Berkshire advertised. I got the job on the first interview and it was just the sort of practice I wanted. There would be four vets; three LA (the boss Andrew Edgson, plus a lovely Irishman called George O'Malley and me) together with the equally Irish and amusing SA vet Dermod Malley. So not only did I go from Woking to Wokingham but into a practice with a Malley and an O'Malley. They both had a wicked twinkle in their eyes and were two of the nicest vets 'you'd meet in a year's travel', as they say over there. At the interview, I was shown the empty flat above the surgery which was going to be mine and by the time I arrived it had been decorated and furnished beautifully. One of the first things that Andrew said to me was that although I was employed as the junior LA assistant, I would have to do a few of Dermod's small animal clinics if he had the afternoon off, plus the operating lists if he was on holiday. But, Andrew said, 'Don't hesitate to ask me if you have any small animal problems, John', which was a bit of a porky pie as he could blag his way through a SA clinic but I never saw him operate on one. On the other hand, he was a top-rate cattle vet. My job was mostly farm but I was asked to try to build up the equine side of the practice, which being my main interest I was delighted to do.

The first day I spent with Andrew (unpaid) on his rounds to see the area and meet some of the farmers, but from the second day I was on my own (and my salary started). He gave me my visit round the next morning and he had included on the list one or two of the farms we had visited the day before. I asked him how to get there. He looked at me absolutely dumbfounded.

'But we went there yesterday.'

'Yes, I know, but we didn't go there directly from here. Anyway I didn't memorise the roads and turnings because a lot of the time we were chatting about the cases we had seen and the way your practice works in general.' Having been born and raised in Wokingham and lived there all his life except when at university, he couldn't at all see how I would think it difficult to find my way around. That was something that cropped up again and again, as I will relate in Chapter 5.

However, with a map and some useful directions from George who had overheard the conversation, I slowly got to know the area. Andrew was like a big teddy bear with horn-rimmed glasses and he spoke like Captain Mainwaring from 'Dad's Army', very brusque and he didn't suffer fools gladly (so I didn't stand a chance). He was single and always seemed to be in a huddle of conversation with his secretary, Jilly. If I had to ask him something first thing in the morning before we went off on our rounds, he would grumpily answer my query and then say: 'Now, Jilly, what were we saying before we were so rudely interrupted?' Yes, he could be pretty offhand but I loved the work, the salary was good, I enjoyed the flat above the surgery and you just put up with these things. I did manage to make the equine side grow and found the balance perfect.

We had trained at Langford under the phenomenal Harold Pearson (then senior lecturer and later professor of surgery), who apart from being an extraordinary surgeon, delivered all his lectures without a note. He had shown us a vast range of surgical techniques, many of them his own creation and he had written heaps of papers, published in the veterinary press.

An example was a new technique of his for correcting uterine torsion in cattle, where the uterus (womb) twists on its axis and it is impossible for the cow to calve. Unless you can sort it out manually you have to operate and one Saturday afternoon Andrew told me to take the caesarean kit to a farm - a cow he had seen that morning - and get on with one. I told him I'd go over and try a couple of techniques first and if they didn't work, I would do the operation. He said no, it's quite impossible, just go and do the c-section as I've told you. I went there first anyway and did manage to correct the torsion following Harold's technique and delivered a live calf. The following Monday morning he asked, 'How did the caesar go, John?' I told him it hadn't been necessary, but do you know, he didn't even compliment me? 'That's all right then,' was all he muttered as he wandered off to find Jilly.

On another weekend I was supposed to be off from Saturday midday but the day before, he said,

'John, you'll have to work this weekend.'

'But Andy, I'm invited to a wedding in Hampshire tomorrow afternoon.'

'Well, you'll just have to miss it.'

'It's your weekend, why can't you do it?'

'I've got some important meetings.'

'This just isn't fair, Andrew.'

'It can't be helped.'

'Andy, I worked last weekend, this is my weekend off. If you start doing this sort of thing, I don't think I'll stay very long.'

THE EARLY YEARS IN PRACTICE

'Oh, all right you can have tomorrow afternoon and evening off, though it's most inconvenient (harrumph) but you must be back here by 6am on Sunday.'

Great, so much for drinks at the reception with all the people I'd know. I drove down to orange juice-fuelled festivities and left at 4.30am to get back in time. I'd been back at the flat no more than ten minutes when the phone rang; a call to see a calf with pneumonia, on a farm I hadn't visited before. They gave me directions and I turned up just as they had started milking. I put my head around the shed door and shouted over the noise of the machinery that it's the vet to see a calf. He said he wouldn't be long and I waited. After hanging around - it was seven on a Sunday morning and I'd only slept two hours on someone's sofa - I went back in.

'Do you want me to see this calf or not?' I asked.

'Oh yeah, sorry, I forgot; I'll get someone.'

The occasion didn't stick in my mind but a week later Andrew said,

'I've had a serious complaint from the owner of Wallsbrook Farm. It seems that you were very high-handed with his dairyman.'

'Oh there... yes, I remember... what exactly did I do wrong?'

'You were rude to him.'

'Was I? Is the calf better?'

'I have no idea, but from now on you are not to go to that farm.'

'Did the farmer say that?'

'Well... erm... you're banned from there, that's all.'

'But I've never been intentionally rude to any of your clients.'

'Well, it can't be helped, I'll have to go myself to Wallsbrook from now on, it's most inconvenient.' (harrumph again).

Such a lovely way to encourage young graduates, Andrew. But six months later I was on call one weekend and had driven rather out of RT (radio telephone) range as I had to take a friend to Heathrow. Wokingham was part of a collection of vet practices, called the 'GP Mayal group' and there wasn't much connection between them except on the RTs at night. These were staffed by a lovely old lady called Mrs Muspratt (George called her 'Mrs. Mousetrap') all night for any vets who were out in their cars.

I was a very minor member of the group and wasn't called much, but one of them was Peter Scott Dunn who was the Queen's horse vet and regularly I would hear 'PSD to the Royal Mews'. As there was no one at my flat when I was out, the only way to be contacted was via the RT, but if you were in your car at night, you were either on your way to a call and couldn't really abandon it for another one, or you were at the call itself in which case you couldn't hear it or answer. Either way, the main benefit of the RT at night was if you were on your way back home, and could turn around.

That night as I got back into RT range returning to the Reading area, Mrs. Muspratt's broad north-country voice chimed, 'Second call to JS, a calving at Wallsbrook Farm, Sherfield.' Which farm? I'd got used to them all by that stage and could find my way to any of them, but that one only rang a slight bell. Ah ... yes, I know what it is, it's that one I'm banned from; this'll be interesting. It was about ten pm when I got there and it was a tricky calving but successful and I was watched by an older farmer, whom I assumed was the boss. Afterwards he said,

'Nice work, young man. Do you want a cup o'tea?'

'Thanks.' Back at the farmhouse he asked,
'I haven't seen you here before, have I?'
'Well, I did come once before.' I told him the story.

'Oh, that was about a six-month ago, wasn't it? I think I remember my dairyman saying something about a young vet being a bit sharp with him - but he's got a memory like a sieve. And I certainly didn't ban you from the farm, that's completely untrue.' And from that day until I left, he insisted that it was *me* and not Andrew, that came and did the work there.

Obstetrics is that branch of gynaecology which deals with, putting it bluntly, getting calves, foals, lambs, piglets and so on, out of their mums and into the air. The subject was well taught at Langford by the reproduction and infertility team I have already mentioned and it's an important part of a LA vet's life. Mares usually foal on their own, for several reasons. One seems to be that they really don't like being observed giving birth to their foals. At the hospital as students, we could wait for ages to witness that magnificent sight and then, thinking she wasn't quite ready, go off to the canteen for a quick coffee to return to her and her brand-new foal. She would always have that knowing sort of '*fooled you, suckers!*' look in her eye, too. The other reason is that foals are very streamlined except in the case of one or two very stocky breeds; they are long and thin and generally slide out pretty easily.

With calves the picture is more mixed. Aiming to increase the volume of beef animals or milk yields of the dairy breeds, attempts over the decades have been made to mix breeds for optimal production. This is usually by artificial insemination and a few drops of frozen semen in a pipette that have been thawed for introduction into the uterus of a small heifer may conceal a big bull. In any case, dystocias (difficult births) are much more commonly encountered in cattle than in horses.

When we are called out to them the first thing is to work out which legs are which, because it is usually the legs that cause the problems. A normal 'presentation' (that is, the way the calf comes up through the pelvis into the vagina) is with the hooves of the two front legs appearing first and the muzzle just behind and above them. Usually, the cow will proceed perfectly normally to deliver the calf in such a presentation, or maybe with a little gentle help from the farmer and we are seldom involved. However, if just one leg appears first (or two legs and no head), that's where obstetrics comes in. We are by that time in a 'calving gown', a rubber tunic that goes down from the neck to almost the ground and a long plastic glove, washed and lubricated. In goes our arm, usually up to the shoulder to try and discover why only one leg or no head has appeared or why the cow is pushing but nothing is presenting at all.

Textbooks have been written on this but the brief story is to try to find, if one leg only is presenting, where its partner is located and to try to bring it up into the vagina. Coming the other way, calves can be born backwards so long as the two hind limbs appear first, but not if the hind limbs are flexed and the 'bottom' is felt first (a 'breech' presentation). The whole thing becomes vastly more complicated when twins are involved, as then you have altogether eight spindly legs to sort out rather than four. In many cases we have to attempt to push the calf *back* into the womb; difficult if she is straining hard and may involve the need for nerve blocks, to get the right limbs to come up first or even to turn the calf around inside completely before it can be delivered.

For all infertility or gynaecological examinations, foaling or calving, we have to be right behind the mare or cow. Cows do not in general kick backwards though they can fetch you a nasty blow sideways if they feel like it. Mares obviously resent their private parts being interfered with; some are kind and placid but others are not and we have to take precautions. In professional studs, special bars are built to allow artificial insemination, pregnancy diagnosis and foaling behind the mares. But all too often in my time this had to be done either with no protection behind at all, or over the top of a half-door. That was fine unless she decided to sink down, taking your arm with her. You were protected from a single hind leg kick (though they made a heck of a rattle on the loose box door) but if she tilted her body forward and kicked back with both legs you were completely exposed. All you could then hope was that the hooves passed each side of your head. I only got a full double hind leg kick once; the left hoof whistled past my ear and the right one shattered the wooden upright of the door frame.

A common sequel of calving is that the placenta (the 'afterbirth') does not completely fall out and it hangs indecorously behind the cow, often to the ground. It has to be removed properly; pulling just breaks it and once again we are up to our shoulder feeling right down into the inside of the uterus slowly detaching the parts of the placenta (the so-called 'cotyledons') from the endometrium. If it is not done properly there is the risk of the remains of the placenta rotting and becoming infected. One of our least favourite procedures.

A big client in Wokingham was REME – the remount depot of the local Cavalry division, schooling horses for largely ceremonial purposes. There were about forty stabled horses or out to pasture in the summer. While I was there, we had two cases of Equine Grass Sickness – a fatal disease whose cause has even now, never been convincingly established. Each case was in a group of horses that had used a particular area to graze and one of the sergeants, who had been with the unit since he joined the army, told me there was an old quarry down there. It had partially filled itself in and was now grazeable, but he remembered being told that a number of horses had been buried there a long time before, of an unknown disease. We went down and had a look and there were no bones to be seen, but knowing that it is a form of dysautonomia where the intestine becomes paralysed, I wondered if there was some infectious agent that had remained there.

But routine bugs would not survive that long, and I forgot about it until I saw a number of cases of Feline Dysautonomia in cats. This entirely new disease, originally called 'Key-Gaskell' syndrome, affected them in an apparently random way from about 1984. The cats became thin and ill, could not swallow and the main finding was a paralysis of the oesophagus and partial paralysis of the upper small intestine. It was caused apparently by damage to the autonomic movement of the gut, hence 'dysautonomia'. Nobody had any idea of the cause and the search for bacteria, viruses, fungi, yeasts and known toxins proved negative. I saw three cases, and the only factor that those had in common, on questioning the owners, was that they had all been given a popular brand of tinned beef-based cat food.

I began to wonder if that was significant and wrote to the *Veterinary Record* on the subject, but my theory was rejected by the couple of academics who responded to it on those pages. They made the point that organisms could not possibly survive the high temperatures involved in processing commercial cat food. But, I wondered, could there be some entirely new disease agent involved here that can persist for years and be eaten? Prions (rogue proteins such as those causing 'mad cow disease' and Jakob-Creutzfeldt syndrome) had not by then been identified, but not being 'living', they can survive long periods and are unaffected by cooking. I have no idea now whether Grass Sickness in horses and Feline Dysautonomia in cats could actually be caused by prions, but it remains a personal theory.

One 'examination' that young vets in practice had to undergo was the one imposed by MAFF involving any official Ministry of Agriculture work such as tuberculin testing (diagnosing the presence of tuberculosis) and blood sampling for brucellosis (a serious infection that causes abortion in cattle and can transmit to humans, in the form of a chronic illness). To be allowed to do these tests, after graduating you needed to become officially an LVI (Local Veterinary Inspector) and were booked to be observed by a ministry vet to prove you can do them properly. Unfortunately, this was a classical 'Catch 22' situation since as a young graduate you haven't had much practice with taking bloods from cattle or giving the tuberculin injections and you need to do lots before you become good at them. But ministry regulations said you were not allowed to do them in an official capacity before you were examined.

In my case, the ministry couldn't fit my exam in for three months, but during that interval Andrew had no choice but to send me out on such calls because they were such a big part of LA practice. Then back at the surgery he had to sign off the tests I had done myself. I entirely confess that we were both acting illegally as far as our strict governing body would have been concerned, but nobody could explain to us how it could be done otherwise.

The exam day arrived and it was on a farm that had been pre-booked where there were both T-testing and brucella bloods to do. I was expecting some old buffer to arrive but the MAFF vet, Owen Porson, was a likeable character and something of an eccentric. After he told me I had 'passed' (well ...), I felt a bit wicked and asked him to show me his own technique. He went a bit pale and then huffed and puffed to raise the jugular vein on another heifer. He did succeed in filling the vacuum tube after a few goes but I could see that his smile afterwards was as much relief as elation.

The SA side of the LVI system involves the examination and certification for pet animals leaving the country. This may or may not involve the rabies vaccine (of which more in a later chapter) but you do have to be LVI. When, years later, I was doing a locum in Bournemouth, clients brought in their young cocker spaniel bitch for the health certificate prior to their emigrating to South Africa. I did the examination, completed the export forms and then rang the ministry to order a rabies vaccine, as we were required to do. The official asked,

'Are you an LVI?'

'Yes.'

'We don't seem to have your name here under that practice.'

'I'm the locum.'

'You're not an official LVI then.'

'I was one in my own practice in Romsey until I recently sold it.'

'Well, you've lost the right to call yourself LVI.'

'How can that be?'

'It's the law, you can't sign documents in Bournemouth.'

I had to explain to the baffled owners that I could not, after all, do the health check and had to ask them to come back when the practice principal returned from holiday. Fortunately, it didn't affect their emigration plans so no harm was done. But it was a waste of time for both of us and after twenty years in practice, I was being told by Defra that I was unqualified to examine a dog and pronounce her fit for the sea journey to sunny South Africa. Mmm.

In Wokingham we had horse clients with two 'Argies'- Argentinian ponies - for polo training. The owners were an unusual couple; he was the proprietor of several highly successful car showrooms and quite a rough diamond. He was a tall and handsome guy but with big red hands and I should imagine he had had a 'challenging' childhood in the London area. His wife was Dutch; short, feisty and very amusing until she lost her temper, which I saw her do several times. They lived in a swanky rural suburb of Wokingham, in an extraordinary, huge log house. Not the so-called 'logs' which are glorified pine planks with which we build our chalets and summer houses. These were full-on debarked trunks, flattened top and bottom and jointed to fit like a jigsaw. The house had been imported as a kit from Canada (in the days before 'carbon footprint' had been invented) and you could imagine the loving couple over there in North America outside a similar house, standing back and admiring their new home. He lifts up his huge lumberjack's chainsaw and says; 'Where d'ya want the doors and windows, honey?'

Nicky, their eighteen-year-old daughter and only child was a complete contrast; shy and well-spoken. She told me that she had been sent to the best girls' school in the area and all the expensive new boxes and equipment were for her. Having started as their vet they seemed to become curiously interested in me; invited me sometimes to dinner and took me as their guest to various equine events. These could be polo competitions if I had an afternoon off, or one evening they drove us up to London for the televised Horse of the Year Show at Wembley.

They were interested in buying a third Argie, for sale at a stud in Dumbarton in Scotland. Could I take the day off and fly up with Nicky, to vet it? That word 'vetting' horses, by the way, means a detailed examination at rest and at exercise and a written report, with a view to purchasing. Her father would pay not only the fee and the airfares but an appropriate sum for the loss of my day's work. I asked Andrew who, trying to seize his chance of an interesting day out, said he would do it himself. He ignored my comment that I thought they wanted me not him, but he was determined to go until he rang Nicky's dad and was told in no uncertain terms to mind his own business. It was me to go up there or nobody.

I must admit I think I was partly being set up; it was not so much a question of my brilliant abilities as an equine vet, as a possible respectable professional man and husband for their daughter. Nicky was beautiful but not my type and I certainly was in no hurry to hear 'papa' say, 'What are your intentions towards my daughter, mate, because I think we should know, shouldn't we?'

I'm sure he had some very ugly friends and being well over six foot, I was not going to make it worse for him by his daughter marrying a short-arse. At the time, though, he did make it fairly obvious and drove us to Heathrow where we flew up on the shuttle. We were met at the airport by the vendor who spoke some sort of Swahili – at least I later worked out that *'Yoodinnee wanttae goo listenin' tae these pokey-*

faced guidfer nothins who dinnae ken one end ae'a horse frae another tellin' yoo yer job' meant that he had confidence in my abilities. In the end I 'spun' the pony having found a few defects so she was not going to buy it, but it was a day with a difference.

One week the circus came to Wokingham and I had been about to buy a ticket for an evening show when they rang and asked for a visit. I was met there by the owner who asked me to tetanus vaccinate his llamas and have a look at a couple of the performing horses. He paid cash on the nail and invited me to lunch with his wife in their caravan. She was surrounded by four very sweet chihuahuas and was a great cook. They fascinated me with stories of their travels and exploits and I had already been impressed by their obvious kindness towards the animals and visible pride in them. They all seemed happy and well-fed and I mused that although it must be a weird life for them with their regular moving on and crossing the country, theirs was a more interesting existence than they might have had in a zoo.

He gave me a ticket for that night's show and as I was leaving, said, 'Oh, could you have a quick look at Nelly?' You guessed it, she was one of the elephants. I'd never been that close to one before and was feeling a bit dense, but she just had a cut on one of her forelegs and the flies were bothering it. It didn't look as if it needed stitching (and I supposed you'd need special heavy-duty needles for a job like that) but should heal by granulation naturally. All it needed was a puffer powder containing an antibiotic for infection and a fly-repellant. That evening I saw him first as the knife-thrower with the poor lady who had cooked my lunch as his 'target' strapped onto a rotating wooden board. Then later I spotted him in another costume with a false beard as the magician, an assistant with the elephants and a scene-shifter. And before the finale, his wife gave her act with her troupe of performing chihuahuas.

With Nelly I had been about to tell him that I had no knowledge of elephants or any other tropical or exotic animal diseases because for those vets specialising in it, there was a post-graduate diploma course in tropical medicine at the University of Edinburgh. In that case, treating Nelly was just using common sense but it made me think about treating species that we were unfamiliar with. All of the pre-clinical years at vet school we had been looking at the anatomy of various species, the way their bodies functioned, the bacteria, viruses, fungi and parasites that could cause disease and non-specific pathology. We then learned how to operate, the basis of surgery, sterile technique, how to put our gloves on without contaminating the outsides; even 'advanced' techniques such as asking your nurse to scratch your nose if it itches or adjust your glasses, as you can't touch them.

And in medicine we had studied in depth all the clinical approaches. I realised on the spot that if Nelly had had something more serious I might, nonetheless, have been able to make some sense of it by just working from 'first principles'. Medicine is medicine in all the species, and surgery, after all, is just 'warm carpentry and plumbing'. If you have a detailed grounding, you could take on exotic species – not as well as an expert of course – but in an urgent case you might be able to cope. Mending, say, a ruptured bowel in an ostrich would be a bit like repairing a lead pipe but with living tissue. Plating or pinning fractures is, in the same way, a bit like mending a chair leg ... alright I've taken the analogies far enough. But if you know *how* to operate - and we did by that time - it's a question of adapting your existing knowledge to a new situation.

I was not supposed to be doing much SA work in

Wokingham outside some clinics if Dermod had an early finish or was on planned leave. But it turned out not to be quite like that; the poor chap had occasional bad migraines and I had to step in at the last minute for him. I would go down to the office in the morning to check on my farm and horse list to be told that instead I must do Dermod's work for the day, including his ops. The clinics I didn't mind but he was an experienced SA surgeon and when I saw his list, my heart would often drop. I would see that several of them were operations I'd never done before and in one or two cases, hardly heard of. I would tear back upstairs to the flat to scrabble through surgery textbooks and read up on the difficult ones, and then get on with the consultations before the ops. It was certainly being thrown into the deep end and although Andy had made that offer, I knew it was pointless asking for his help.

The other Irishman, George O'Malley, had entered practice in England via a curious route. He was as Irish as soda bread to look at and speak to, but it turned out that his family had emigrated to Argentina when he was a child. He had got his vet degree at the University of Buenos Aires, so he had been taught entirely in Spanish. He occasionally got his English a bit confused and any word he was searching for was inevitably preceded by, 'You know… the auld… a bit of the auld…', so he'd suggest, 'Give it a bit of the auld, you know, the auld… antibiotics.' Or when we were together doing my first bovine caesarean in practice (I had seen them done at Langford but had never attempted one on my own) and as he supervised me, he said 'Use the auld… you know… the auld canife.' He meant the scalpel of course.

George had remarked when we met that having left Argentina, in order to practice in the UK he had had to pass the British professional exams as his Argentinian qualification was not accepted and he said that it was like going through vet school twice.

In the end I must have done forty or so bovine caesareans in Wokingham and it became quite routine. Incidentally, the word caesarean comes from the Latin for 'cut' ('caedere; caesum') rather than from the Roman Julius Caesar, though it's possible that he was born that way. However, his mother lived and the operation was in those days only done on women who had died, to save the baby. 'Caesar' (from a different root) became used to represent 'King', as in 'Kaiser', 'Tzar' or 'Czar'.

In any case it's now almost always shortened to 'do a caesar', and they seemed to be mostly in the evenings around 10pm, usually because the farmer had been trying to calve her for a few hours himself and would ring us before bedtime. They are nearly always done with the cow standing and a flank incision (on the side of the abdomen) under local anaesthetic. It is possible under general anaesthesia in certain conditions but of course the calf becomes partially anaesthetised too and breathing can be compromised. One can also try epidural spinal block but the cow will not be able to remain standing, as her hind legs will become paralysed. In any of those cases if she has to (or decides to) lie down you can still carry on with it so long as your incision remains accessible, but it is generally much easier if she remains standing.

When I was doing them, the word would often get around to the farm staff and neighbours that a c-section was going on and they would all troop over to watch. I would get used to hearing over my back the usual ribald comments in broad Berkshire accents about 'A lovely bit o'steak there, moosh' as I cut through muscle, and would wait for the first one to drop. They were all behind me so I couldn't see them, but yes... crash... as one went down and was carried out. I almost did a sweepstake in my head as to how many minutes would elapse before the first one fainted; it was true that bovine caesars were pretty gory. Whether today's farmers could afford the high fee of such an operation with their perilously slim profit margins is anyone's guess.

George had two enormous Irish Wolfhounds which he regularly had in the Range Rover with him on his farm calls. He and his wife Moira and their three daughters lived with them in a semi-detached house and the dogs pretty well filled it. I was invited to dinner a few times and we always sat in the small dining room around the table for the whole evening while the dogs sprawled over the sofas in the living room. George only did LA work but it wasn't rare to be asked about SA things and one day a farmer's wife asked him to look at a pair of young guinea pigs with some sort of mange (a skin disease). He said he'd take them back to the surgery in a wicker basket for Dermod to examine. Trouble was they didn't arrive. When he got back to Wokingham the cage door was open and they were nowhere to be seen. He searched the car high and low; in corners, under the seats and emptied all his medical equipment out, but they were just not there. The Wolfhounds watched him doing it, looking guilty and quietly smacking their chops. George came clean to the farming family and bought them two replacements that didn't have sarcoptic mange so everyone was happy including the dogs.

A bovine operation we had to do occasionally was a rumenotomy; that is, opening the rumen (the massive main stomach) to retrieve a 'foreign body', some object – usually metallic - that the cow had mistakenly eaten and which, causing pain, resulted in its looking ill and losing weight. This is an operation seldom done these days as, again, the value of the animal's dead carcass must be assessed relative to the vet's charges for the operation, and it does take them some time to recover from it. But in the case of a very valuable animal or a family pet (such as the 'house cow') we would occasionally do them.

What was surprising was how HOT the contents of the rumen were when you opened it; almost too hot to touch. It took me back to when I was a teenager and helping an uncle empty his blocked septic tank. The connection between the two might seem a bit weird, but bear with me here. He lowered a waterproof pump into the bottom of the tank and we pumped the contents onto a field via a long pipe. It was in the middle of winter, and with me on the far end of the pipe I couldn't believe how the liquid passing through it was warming up my chilled fingers.

Very much the same process is happening in a cow's rumen as happens in the biological process within a septic tank. Bacteria and other micro-organisms are converting organic matter into digestible food, with the simultaneous production of large quantities of heat. The rumen, the second stomach in cattle after the reticulum and before the omasum and abomasum, has a volume of around 150 litres. It needs to be that large in order that the otherwise indigestible cellulose which is the bulk of what cattle eat, is converted into useful food. And it also explained something that I couldn't understand before I was a student; that on freezing winter days why is it that cattle remain so warm to the touch? How do they survive when outside through the winter with such short coats? The simple answer is that the rumen is their internal 'furnace' to keep them warm in cold weather.

Sheep are also ruminants, though in a slightly different way so they have their own 'central heating' as well as their wool in the cold months. Horses manage to keep warm outside with a combination of that process and their winter coats, though in their case the 'fermentation' is not in a rumen, but in their caecum (a huge part of the large intestine and about thirty litres in volume). We still have the tiny remains of a caecum; our appendix.

It also explains why cattle's abdomens are so pendulous as most of those 150 litres are at the bottom, of course. And for breeding cows, they have to find the additional space for a surprisingly large calf, once it is close to being born. It's the reason why it is seldom clear whether a cow is in calf or not in the early stages. We have to pull on those long plastic gloves again, go into the rectum and feel for the uterus underneath; the ubiquitous Pregnancy Diagnoses (PDs).

We had a major contract where I did hundreds of PDs a year, at the NIRD (National Institute for Research into Dairying) at Arborfield, Berkshire, a huge spread with a thousand milking cows. One day there I had just finished some S19 (brucellosis) vaccines for a batch of calves when one of the men shouted 'Quick, get the vet, a cow is choking!' They had been experimenting with feed compacted into different-sized 'boluses' to see if they were more digestible than the loose stuff.

This cow had got one lodged against her larynx and was down on the concrete floor, unable to breathe and close to death. I tried using an instrument to get it out without success, so all I could do was put my left hand deep down into her throat. I felt the obstruction but, being rounded and covered in slippery saliva, I couldn't at first get hold of it. Eventually, by trying with my nails I got a grip on it and pulled it out.

As the cow felt that the obstruction was gone, she closed her open mouth and crunched down onto my thumb between her molar teeth with those powerful masseter muscles. She then got up but I didn't. With the pasty white remains of a thumb (it was so mashed that it didn't even bleed at first, but later it poured) I felt a bit faint but bandaged it myself and was given some tea. I really didn't feel like completing my round and the only call left at that end of the afternoon was for about thirty PDs at a different farm, so I rang the practice and told Andy what had happened.

'Take care of yourself, John, I'll see you in about an hour and a half.'

'An hour and a half?'

'Well, you're going to do those PDs, aren't you?'

'I thought you might be able to step in.'

'No, I've got too much on.' Another tête-à-tête with Jilly I should think. So I had no choice but to go and do them right-handed - I was normally left-handed but had that one bound up. I got back to the surgery and had forgotten that it was Dermod's evening off and I had to do his SA clinic with one hand too. Andy had gone home; all good for the character, I'm sure.

The thumb healed up in about a month (though it took a year for the nail to grow again) and I re-dressed it daily while continuing work. I didn't have a GP doctor, though I met a most unusual version of one in the form of a client. Marguerite de Beaumont was an erudite and fascinating old lady who owned Shalbourne Manor on the Berkshire/Wiltshire border. It was a huge sixteenth-century Elizabethan house, together with its accompanying stud which was beautifully designed, built with the best materials and run by a very competent groom. I took immediately to Marguerite when I started doing her veterinary work, driving the long distance from Wokingham. She always invited me for tea afterwards and I tried to organise my visits there as the last call of the day when I was not doing the out-of-hours, so I could spend part of an evening with her.

She and her sister - with whom she shared their home - had never married; she had so many stories to tell and knew horse management inside out. She taught me a lot and gave me a signed copy of her book, 'The Way of a Horse'; full of good equine tips and I still have it in my library. She was too modest to tell me that she had been a close friend of Lord Baden-Powell and she had founded the Girl Guide movement (I discovered that later) but she did recount the tale of her becoming the 'GP' at Shalbourne, during the war.

The proper doctor had gone off to serve in the army and although she was not medically qualified, she was clearly highly educated and was asked by the village council to open a surgery in one of the offices at the Manor. There she did a sort of 'triage'; giving sensible advice and guidance to some patients, dishing out aspirin, poultices, splints, creams or dressings to others, and in the case of anything she thought might be more serious, telling them to find their way to the hospital in Hungerford four miles away. When she died in 1989, she left the Manor and the whole estate to her new vet, Philip Pocock, a colleague whom I knew vaguely. It would have been me, I suppose; if I hadn't moved on, but I am glad that I eventually did.

Apart from Marguerite, we by then had several clients around the Newbury/Thatcham direction including a couple of riding schools and a National Hunt yard, so I was often on the M4 from Wokingham. As a teenager I had hitch-hiked a lot; coming from Devon or Cornwall you had to hitch everywhere because families often couldn't afford a car – we certainly didn't have one. So if I ever saw someone looking reasonable wanting a lift, I would pick them up if I could.

One morning, arriving at my usual junction 10 heading west, I saw what appeared at first to be a spectral vision. A girl, looking like an angel, in a long white flowing dress and without luggage or even a handbag was standing at the junction roundabout, alone and with her thumb out. I blinked, saw that it was real, pulled up and she asked if I was going to Newbury. I replied yes and she got in. She was highly intelligent and I was quite concerned for her. Why was she hitch-hiking? Was she in any trouble? No, she said, she just suddenly needed to get to Newbury.

In her turn she asked me quite a lot of questions, but I was disconcerted as she seemed to be regularly looking over her shoulder, behind us. Was she being pursued by someone unwelcome? She asked to be dropped off on the roundabout of junction 13 and, quite worried for her, I offered to take her to a safer place such as the centre of Newbury. But she said no thank you, she wanted to be left on the roundabout. I dropped her off there with misgivings but had forgotten all about it until one evening when George came up to my flat.

'What's this about you picking up girls on the M4?'

'What do you mean?'

'You're in the local paper.'

'What?!'

'Did you pick up a girl on her own in a white dress?'

'Er... yes, I did... oh God... what's happened?'

'She was a reporter from the Reading evening paper and there are two photos of the back of your car and her getting in.'

I went out and bought the newspaper and it was true, there was a double-page spread. She had been doing a piece on hitchhiking and had been chaperoned by another reporter in his car, together with a photographer. In her article she wrote, '... *but by that time I'd lost my escort because I was picked up by a young vet on his way to Thatcham and he drove so fast that we lost them and from then on, I was on my own.'* To judge by her piece, she must have been a real reporter but I'd prefer to remember her as an angel.

In any case Wokingham had been great experience for me, and thank you, Messrs. Malley and O'Malley, if you're reading this, for your support over those eighteen months. Even though the SA operating unsupervised was a complete nightmare at the time, it was invaluable. I had been looking at my career and experience so far and recognised that although Andy was a good farm vet and was paying me well, he was too irascible to consider staying much longer. And in that period I had squeezed a lot of experience both SA and LA into a short time. Although it was not the normal procedure to 'go solo' after two years, I began to think that I was ready for it. Most vets tended to remain with their first or second jobs and then buy into the practice to become a partner, but I fancied putting up my plate on my own. But where?

Chapter 3

Romsey

My accountancy student friend Jim and his girlfriend Pat had bought a house in Romsey in southern Hampshire and although they married and emigrated to Australia soon after, it was an introduction to that old market town of, then, about 13,000 inhabitants. So during some holidays from Wokingham, I was looking around for potential premises to convert into a surgery. My mum, after a long period as a widow, had remarried and my new step-father's job was in Southampton. She moved there and it was on a visit to her and to Jim that I had a chance to have a closer view of Romsey. It was a busy little market town dominated by the enormous Strong's brewery (which became Whitbread Strong's) churning out beer for most of Hampshire and beyond.

There was a saying around the town, 'So drunk he must have been to Romsey', and the local history group published a book with that title. They tracked down over eighty named pubs that had existed in Romsey during the nineteenth and twentieth centuries. This was in addition to many known simply as 'beer sellers', who got a licence and opened their front room to make a bit of extra money. The group estimated that in 1911 there had been a pub for every 141 inhabitants; if there were the same ratio to the current population of Romsey there would now be over a hundred pubs there. Beer, having been boiled, was safer than water or fresh milk to drink and better for people than 'Madame Geneva'; its competitor, gin, so its sale was officially encouraged. It also brought wealth to the town (on top of the wool trade) from Excise on the beer, the sale of licences and the increasingly prosperous breweries. Many publicans had in the past brewed their own beer but by the twentieth century the breweries had taken over, and bought up many of the pubs, to become 'tied houses'. The most successful brewer (and the town's biggest employer) was Strong and Company, Romsey, which was later bought by Whitbread Wessex Ltd.

It was a popular and growing town; there was only one other veterinary practice, and even that was part-time (a branch of a large and old-established practice in Southampton). It was also interesting as it had a big catchment area, lying roughly in the middle of a triangle between Southampton, Winchester and Salisbury. Consequently, I was looking for premises preferably on the edge of town and easy to access from outside, rather than getting caught up in traffic around the centre, where the other practice was.

Then I saw the 'Horse and Jockey', a closed Whitbread Strong's pub dating from the eighteenth century, lying on the western edge of Romsey on the intersection between the roads to Salisbury and the West. I happened across an old photo of the pub in its prime and it had had an enormous oil painting of a horse and its jockey mounted on the outside front wall but that had been taken down, though the old pub lettering remained on another wall. Blackened with road dust and locked up, it seemed an ideal spot with a large car park and, although it had a noisy main road going past it, it was otherwise perfect. Quite a lot of the pubs in Romsey had closed during the sixties and seventies as it became more difficult to make a profit with increasing brewery rents, rates and legislation involving access to premises, cleanliness and environmental health. I did go and look at the outside of two other closed pubs, but the Horse and Jockey was the one I wanted.

I made an appointment with the Whitbread estates manager for Hampshire; a very friendly and helpful bloke called Tony Barker and we met on site. The property definitely was not for sale, he said, as the Whitbread Board felt that they may have a use for it in the future; though not, he thought, within the next ten years. That was good news for me as I had almost no money of my own, and if I started a practice from scratch with no guarantee that it would become successful or financially viable, who would lend me any? Without the certainty that I would be able to repay a mortgage, no banks or building societies were going to be very interested. Mum had said she would lend me some, but nothing like the sums necessary to buy and restore such a big place even as a deposit, as internally the property was very shabby in parts and almost ruined in others.

There was no hot water except for a small gas heater and hot tap in the bar area (though I noted that at least there was mains gas and it was still connected, as was the electricity and water). Elsewhere in the property there was no heating, plumbing or electric cabling. The old couple who had been the tenants apparently lived in one of the grotty upstairs rooms (using lamplight or candles, I supposed). Another rumour I heard was that they were pretty rude to the customers in general and I gathered that on the day they decided to close it for good, the locals turned up at lunchtime for their pints, found it shut and hammered on the door. A window opened above and 'Mine Host' bellowed,

'Whaddya want?'

'Well… a drink,' they replied.

'Get lost, we're shut,' was apparently the retort (except he didn't say 'get lost', as I had heard from one of those customers). I did meet him once and asked why there hadn't been a bath in the house. 'Only dirty people need baths,' was his gruff reply. Well, the big questions were these:

- Was there some way in which I could lease the premises, as I could not possibly raise the funds to buy it even if it were for sale?
- With only two years of experience as a young vet, was I up to running my own practice?
- Did I have any commercial or business experience?
- What about the existing practice in Romsey?
- How much would repair and restoration cost and how much of it could I do myself?
- What does it cost to buy all the equipment and drug stocks when you start a practice from scratch?
- What sort of legal or administrative procedures are necessary?
- Do I need to inform the Inland Revenue?
- What do I do about accounting and VAT?

The answers slowly became clearer. Tony Barker got back to me and said that he had raised the matter of the Horse and Jockey at a recent Board meeting. They were willing to offer me a ten-year lease on the property provided I carried out all the repairs and restoration necessary, at my own expense. It was a listed building (grade two) but so long as I didn't change it externally, I could do what I liked. I had assumed that in addition, this would entail an annual rent of some sort but he said, 'Oh no, just nominal, a pound or five pounds a year.' This was very good as I had in the interim obtained the option of a small loan from the Romsey branch of the Midland Bank and mum said she could match that, so I reckoned that I could get parts of it done by tradesmen and, with some help, do the rest myself.

To the second question, I was confident in a way that I always have been and frequently against the odds (some would call it reckless). The bar area – most of the ground floor - was ideal in terms of size but it would have to be gutted and completely re-thought. Behind, the rest of that floor was where they had stored barrels and there were even huge hooks bolted to the eighteenth-century beams where I suppose they had hung cured hams, or maybe even poached pheasants or roadkill.

This area would become my first kennels. Upstairs there were two further floors with altogether eight rooms, some in reasonable condition and just needed painting and decorating and the rest were pretty bad with the walls crumbling through damp and neglect. At the very top, the attic rooms had obviously not been inhabited in living memory as any plaster that there had been had fallen off and the floors were covered in twigs, rubble and old birds' nests. The slate roof was intact and it was obvious that the outside parts visible to the general public had been reasonably well maintained by the brewery but not the inside, invisible areas. Much later I had all those slates removed and replaced by old tiles which better reflected the original roofing material. So overall, although it was a huge and scary project with so many potential pitfalls – the worst being that it would never get off the ground - I thought I could make a fist of it having had that baptism of fire in Wokingham and maybe it wouldn't be worse than that.

To the third question, the answer was certainly that I had absolutely no commercial or business experience. But Jim was at the time revising for his chartered accountancy finals and we spent several evenings over pints, with him explaining how to run a business such as mine from an accountant's point of view, and emphasized how important it was to keep good records. He bought me a large double-entry ledger that he said was essential and showed me how to fill everything in. On the left side went the 'Incomings', that is, the fees received, and the larger right-hand side was divided into all the 'Outgoings'; drug bills, staff salaries, gas and electricity, insurance, rates, repairs and renewals, capital equipment purchased, car, fuel and garage bills, miscellaneous/petty cash, income tax and on the far right, VAT.

All veterinary services are subject to VAT and it is a routine now, but at the time the tax had just been introduced and I wasn't the only business owner who would be struggling to understand it. It had been announced by the Chancellor of the period as a 'luxury' tax only, emanating from the EU and in all probability, he claimed at the time, would only be temporary (as if…). But I have to congratulate whoever thought up the term 'Value Added Tax'. What a superb phrase! It gave us 'Value', didn't it? And it was 'Added' too! What a bonus! We not only got 'Value' for our taxes, but cash was 'Added' as well! We were all going to be rich.

The truth was that it was just a tax to raise the funds to support the huge EU budget and dish out millions to large landowners across Europe in the form of massive subsidies to produce arable crops or leave their land fallow. Suddenly brand-new mega-tractors, combine harvesters, seed drills and all the other forms of farm equipment started trundling along the roads of Europe, replacing the antique machinery. Based in Brussels, Luxembourg and Strasbourg they didn't have any real loyalty to British farmers, though the UK politicians tried to fight our corner. In the end we had to rather grumpily accept that as vets we were 'unpaid tax collectors'. The VAT rate was at that time 7.5 per cent and paid over to Customs and Excise every three months. Once I got used to it, it was fairly simple to complete the books but it involved several evenings every quarter down in the office.

The part-time vet practice in Romsey was run by a kindly and well-respected chap called Ralph Proverbs, a white Barbadian vet, and several people told me that they were amazed that I was even dreaming of setting up against such well-established 'opposition'. He had come to the UK to study at Edinburgh vet school and his wife was also a vet but she told me she had lost her nerve after graduating and had since acted as his receptionist and nurse. Several local people swore to me that I'd never make a go of things against him, but I had a couple of aces up my sleeve. He worked primarily from Southampton; his small branch in Romsey had only been open on certain days and times a week and I could see already that a town of that size deserved much better (though they did promptly switch to full-time when they heard about me).

I also established that he disliked operating and apart from very minor surgery, most cases were put into a van in baskets and cages and driven the eight miles to Southampton for surgical jobs. That sort of travelling really is not perfect for stressed animals either pre- or post-operatively. I never briefed against him or told animal owners that being put into a strange vehicle was not ideal, but one would have to accept that the risks of haemorrhage and shock post-operatively were more likely. All of the operating at my practice was going to be done there, and by me. On the other hand, I did like them when I invited them over for coffee to explain my intentions, and they seemed to realise that a second practice in Romsey was both necessary and inevitable.

Having signed the documents, the property was mine for ten years and loyal friends turned up at weekends to help and initiate me into some of the building trades. We demolished most of the two bar areas and partitioned them off in an entirely new pattern with concrete blocks. Then followed a cheap plasterer working in the evenings for cash to skim the blocks with a thin layer of mortar and a week later, a coat of grey plaster. I found a good plumber who was looking for work to install gas central heating and plumbing through the house and a local electrician put in the cabling. I spent my days and evenings painting and decorating, building the kennels myself using concrete blocks again and lining them with ceramic tiles bought as a cheap job lot (the plain ones that I needed didn't sell as well as the decorated ones) and buying up equipment and instruments both new and second hand.

My strip lighting came from a local dentist who was installing spot lamps (kit like that was relatively expensive in those days, before the explosion of big DIY outlets). I bought another job lot of thick vinyl and laid the floors and an old hydraulic dentist's chair base for which a metalworker friend made an inclinable aluminium top, for the operating table. My anaesthetic apparatus was an ex-hospital Boyle's machine that was still perfectly serviceable, with fluothane and racks for oxygen, carbon dioxide and nitrous oxide.

There was an ex-army X-ray machine which I bought very cheaply and to which I will refer later, and the rest of the equipment was new. By the time I officially opened the practice in November 1973 with a small group of friends and some cheap bubbly, my loans had been spent and now I needed clients, rather desperately.

In those days any advertising was entirely prohibited on professional grounds and, as the saying went, 'You screw your plate onto the wall and you sit and wait.' No advert was permitted in any of the local newspapers that you had opened your practice, however discrete and professionally worded, let alone flyers or any of the modern ways of drawing attention to a new business. There were only two things I could do to show that the clinic was open at all. The first was to stick black plastic letters onto the inside of the glass entrance door with the word 'SURGERY' in capitals though this was only visible after dark and the lights were on. The other was a little riskier, and involved the car park outside. Having been a pub it was an excellent parking area with space for about fifteen cars whereas Ralph's practice, right in the centre of town had a tiny car park with very narrow access (I'd checked) so some of his clients had to park as close as possible in town and walk. In most cases that would be feasible but when a very ill animal is brought in and needs to be carried, it is not ideal and in the case of large breeds, very difficult indeed.

I took a chance and had a large, good-quality external sign made, saying *VETERINARY SURGERY. CAR PARKING FOR CLIENTS ONLY.* It was technically 'illegal' in a professional sense, as it could constitute advertising, although I thought it reasonable in that it was mine and not available for public parking. The Southampton practice was quick to write complaining bitterly about it but I refused to remove it and it gave me the advantage of knowing that they were rattled by my arrival. Apart from speaking to Ralph, I had also written formally to all the other practices within the area advising them that I had put up my plate, as one was expected to do. Most wrote back wishing me luck, but the letter from Southampton said, *'Whilst in a professional sense we extend to you the routine courtesies, you must understand that there can be no question of any cooperation between the two practices or any notion of mutual assistance, particularly at night and weekend'*. Fair enough, and once again I was encouraged by their coldness.

One of the advantages that young vets had when they established a practice from nothing was that you wrote in advance to all the pharmaceutical companies, announcing that you were starting up and then most of them sent you a huge box of free samples of all the meds in their range. The idea was firmly commercial as well as being a friendly (and almost essential) gesture as many of the more established pharmaceuticals were manufactured or imported by multiple companies. Therefore, the presumption was that if you started using, for example, Glaxo's amoxicillin you would continue to use and re-order it. This particularly applied to vaccines, whether canine, feline or equine. Most of the major companies sold them and there really wasn't much to tell between them so once again, the vaccines you started using (both because they were effective and easily administered as well as in recognition of the company that donated them to you), you continued to order.

In the first two days of the practice nothing happened (well, hardly anybody knew about it) but about nine on the third morning the practice bell rang and I went down in painting overalls expecting to see the postman. No post, but sitting quietly in the waiting room was a man with a puppy on his lap.

My first client. I had just put my head around the door and I don't think he saw the overalls, but I dashed upstairs, changed, put on a blue tunic, and did the first vaccination in my own right. Of course, this involves a health check, advice about feeding, worming and general care for inexperienced owners, and I was on my way.

The loans from the bank and mum had seen me through and I was able to repay her within a year and the Midland a bit later. Every day a few more clients arrived and I quickly took on my first nurse, Moz. I think she may have been called Maureen but hated that name and she proved tremendous. She was unqualified (and therefore cheaper to employ – money was very tight); I trained her and she became highly competent. She had come from another part of England and owned a pony too, so she needed accommodation and a paddock. I had the latter as the land was divided into the surgery and main house, the car park, a garden full of weeds and a decent-sized paddock. I bought her a cheap mobile home - rather on its last legs - and put it in the garden, dug a trench to give her water and electricity and she was very happy there for several years.

By the end of the third month, I would expect maybe three clients in the morning, perhaps a few ops and no more than four or five cases in the evening. But I had LA work and one day needed to go to vet a horse for purchase at the big stables of the Coates family, near Lymington. Ralph Coates' daughter Marion was quite famous as part of the British equestrian team and I had seen her on TV competing on her surprisingly diminutive showjumper 'Stroller'. All equines were measured in 'hands' (a hand being four inches) and we used a special graduated measuring stick of their height from the ground to the top of the shoulder. At a mere fourteen hands two inches,

Stroller was technically only a pony, but with Marion on top had beaten some of the best large thoroughbred jumpers in the world. I felt flattered to be at such an important yard and to be introduced to 'the little feller' as they called him, as he was by then retired.

They took in equestrian students there for their training in Horse Master and Assistant Instructor exams and so quite a gaggle formed around us as I examined the eventer my client was hoping to buy. Just as I finished, someone shouted outside, 'One of the mares has collapsed! Get the vet!' By the time I got to the box she was dead, and Marion asked me what I thought may have been the cause of death. There didn't seem to be any exterior signs and I of course replied that it would need a post-mortem. Although I was not her vet, she asked me if I would do one there and then, partly as a training exercise for the students.

My watch said it was 4pm and I was three-quarters of an hour away from the surgery. But we were still on open surgeries without appointments (the evening one from five to seven pm) and I reflected that at most I would only let two or three people down, as a full horse PM takes an hour. The cause of death was a heart valve defect and later I was driving back down the hill to the practice when I couldn't believe my eyes. On that day – that very day – and completely out of the blue, by 5.45pm on the car clock I could see that the car park was packed full and there were even cars parked on the verge. Moz was desperate (no mobile phones) and I rushed in, not only embarrassed but flabbergasted. We gave most of the owners specific appointments to come back later that evening after their dinner and I happily worked until ten, but for those who were prepared to wait, I got through them as fast as I could and they were all very understanding about it. I probably saw thirty cases but don't think more than six arrived the evening after. Somebody's law, I suppose.

Nurses are the heart and soul of our veterinary practices and I would thoroughly recommend the profession for those girls (or boys, sometimes) who couldn't quite achieve the results to get into vet school. Over the years I had a wonderful succession of them. My second nurse was Jo Warwick-Haller from a prominent family in the New Forest at Minstead. They used the Southampton practice for their own horses and when her dad mentioned to the vet that Jo had just started working for me, he apparently said, 'Well, if she doesn't like it there, I'll make sure she gets a job with us.' Her dad replied, 'She did have an interview with you and you turned her down.' Another example of their wishing I was dead. Jo was a fantastic and intelligent nurse who learned the job quickly and became irreplaceable. She even met her future husband there; he was a pharmaceutical rep and I noticed that he called rather more frequently than most did, and I mentioned it to Jo. She said, 'Yes, he's called Roger and he's just asked me out.' I was invited to their wedding and I bumped into Jo many years later; they were still happy and had a family.

I had gone up to two nurses when one of them gave in her notice as she was getting married. I put a small ad into the jobs section of the Southern Evening Echo newspaper, and that evening was inundated with calls. I would filter the replies mostly on the basis of their responses to my questions and particularly on who sounded pleasant on the phone. An important part of a nurse's job is giving appointments or advice to animal owners when they ring, so their voice is the first impression that a new client would have of the practice.

I then narrowed it down to a shortlist of five or six and interviewed those. On that occasion I finally offered the job to an RVN (Registered Veterinary Nurse) who had already undergone the three-year training. I had a personal policy that I would not employ any nurse whom I might find attractive as I'm ashamed to say I knew myself too well (these are supposed to be stories about the naked truth, aren't they?). Of that shortlist I easily chose the best, a few inches taller than me and she seemed the ideal choice.

Then a week later another girl rang, telling me that a friend of hers had just seen the advertisement – was she too late? She desperately wanted to become a veterinary nurse and had always done so, she said. She didn't have much in the way of qualifications but she told me that she had lived and worked with animals all her life particularly dogs and horses and was a competent rider. This indeed was a big plus in her case and she also had a lovely voice on the phone. But I told her I was very sorry and the post had been filled. She sounded incredibly disappointed, then hesitated and said, 'Look, I know I haven't got the job but I'd really love to have the experience of being interviewed by a vet; would you be willing to give me a dummy interview anyway?' I thought that was enterprising of her and agreed, giving her a time after the end of work one day.

Life and the busy practice went on and I completely forgot about my promise until a week later when, at the end of an evening surgery, walking back through the waiting room with no record cards left in my hand, I saw a lovely girl with long blond hair quietly sitting there, without an animal.

'Er, and you are?'

'Hello, I'm Dawn; you offered to interview me.' Phew! Good job I'd given the job to someone else. The interview was fine, she told me more about her own animals and she was obviously well-connected with stables, kennels, breeders and the like in the Southampton area. We chatted and she left. Two days later, the RVN to whom I'd given the job rang.

'I'm so sorry, this is really embarrassing, but I had two interviews; yours and another, and the second practice has now also offered me a job. I'm going to have to say no to you after all – I apologise for letting you down.'

'Oh, that's difficult, I've already written to all the shortlist saying the post is filled.'

'I realise it's very unprofessional but the other practice is within walking distance of my family home rather than a six-mile drive.'

'Fair enough. Yes of course I understand.'

I was busy and in spare moments was beginning to think of the chore of re-contacting the shortlist for second interviews but out of the blue Dawn rang again and said how grateful she was to have been interviewed… and… she supposed nothing had changed about the job? Well, she was perfect; I really couldn't be bothered to get back to the others, none of whom were as good. She was available to start immediately so that she could spend some time in parallel with the nurse who was leaving two weeks later. The decision was easy. She turned out to be one of the best nurses I ever had; she was already expert at handling animals, learned quickly all the rest of the work and was invaluable coming on horse calls especially surgical jobs as she managed horses effortlessly. She took over as the second nurse, got on well with Sally the qualified RVN who, with me, started training her and she was popular with the clients. We formed a perfect team.

She knew a lot of dog breeders and once invited me to a breeders' meeting in Bournemouth, where I was unknown. She had told me to keep my mouth shut about being a vet and I wondered why. 'You'll see', she said. It was quite a weird sensation; I felt I had always got on with my breeder clients though I was careful not to patronise them. The income from them is important to all SA practices, but I thought it sometimes made them bossy and over-demanding so I tried to find a balance between treating them well, yet not being over-familiar. An excellent breeder of Basset hounds, Mrs. Rowett-Johns was also an astute businesswoman, but I felt that she was becoming a little bit unreasonable. All breeders got a twenty per cent discount, others demanded more but she not only did that, but expected a couple of months to pay her bills. So, I hit on the idea that, 'You can have discount or you can have credit, but you can't have both', and from then on, all the breeders seemed to accept that this was fair.

At the breeders' meeting I was appalled; all they seemed to have to talk about was how rubbish their vets were and how much they wanted to get rid of them. I couldn't understand it at all.

'Don't you see?' Dawn asked when we were driving home.

'They wanted to be vets, and breeding is the nearest thing to it. It's such a pity because they're so good at what they do and I've never understood why they have such a down on the profession.' It was true; they knew much more than I did about selection within their breeds, the mating process itself, management of pregnancy and litters and all of them were good at manual assistance during whelping.

Some of them liked us, though. One breeder of Great Danes, Jean Lanning, had a fantastic range of kennels in the open air at Dunwood Beeches. Some breeders' premises were rather poky but these were sturdy, well-built outside kennels with huge exercise areas ideal for a large breed. I thought her set-up was excellent and was her vet for a long time. I had to do one or two Great Dane spays (a bigger operating table would have been helpful) and caesariens for her, but most whelped naturally. I also regularly went up to batch-vaccinate substantial numbers of puppies, which despite the hefty discount, was highly lucrative as it was the best possible use of a vet's time. And she always gave me a cheque on the spot, which was rare.

She had mentioned to Sally on the phone for one such visit that one of the pups would need a rabies vaccine on top of the routine DHLP inoculation (distemper, hepatitis, leptospirosis and parvovirus) as it was being exported to Germany, could I do the two at the same time? I wasn't sure and rang the vaccine manufacturer who said that while it was always preferable to give them separately, in the case of a rush job they felt that no harm would come of giving the two together, as DHLP was already a multiple vaccine.

However, someone later told Miss Lanning that I should not have given the two vaccines on the same day and instead of ringing me, for some reason she got her solicitor to send me a letter. It was not only the sole legal complaint to the practice I ever received, but it was also illiterate. Typewriters had not quite moved on to word processors with a separate printer, but there were already good makes available to buy, giving quite a professional effect and were already in use by businesses. One brand had a rotating 'ball' instead of the line of keys and produced a decent letter, and I had a make that had a prototype small 'liquid crystal' screen incorporated. You typed a few lines, read the screen to check for errors and then pressed a button whereupon that section was typed out rapidly.

This legal letter must have been knocked out on some redundant World War Two machine, maybe bought second-hand from Bletchley Park, with worn-out letters and apparently an ink tape that had gone backwards and forwards for decades. The lettering was wobbly or out of place, some characters were completely missing, some were bluish, some blackish and some reddish and the words I could discern were mostly misspelled. I smiled at this extraordinary document and posted it on to Miss Lanning, writing that I didn't at all mind if she wanted to change vets but could I recommend she also changed solicitors? She saw the funny side of it and all was well. Breeders came and went and some suddenly disappeared - two of them owing us a lot of money - and I got the impression that they did switch practices fairly regularly (well, we were all useless, weren't we?), but there were some real characters among them.

As far as 'bad debts' were concerned, I dare say we should have been more cynical about fees and insisted that some clients pay a deposit or the full fee upfront, particularly those that were unknown to us. With all the regular clients we might do occasional house calls so their address was confirmed but we discovered that some others gave false addresses, then ran up a bill and we never saw them again. One particularly galling example was new clients who were publicans from a hostelry at Whiteparish between Romsey and Salisbury who booked in two German Shepherd bitches for spaying on the same day. They were guard dogs for the pub; nasty creatures and my nurses put themselves in some danger.

The owners apparently said they would pay when they came back for stitches, then seemingly took them out themselves and ignored our bills. I was tempted to book a lunch up there for myself and a crowd of friends one day and then tell them that they could take the bill out of what they owed me. Many of them, of course, owed money to other practices and were 'doing the rounds' and I did discuss creating a 'black list' with some other local practices but they were concerned over confidentiality issues. My estimate was overall that about five per cent of our accounts remained unpaid but that was probably par for the course for small businesses. To any client that claimed, after their consultation or operation, that they had neglected to bring their cheque books and 'would call by later', there didn't seem much we could do other than agree. Since then, I know that practices are much firmer, and with credit card payments less clients can claim to have 'forgotten'.

Among breeders, another such free spirit was Mrs. Leavy, who worked in quite a different way. An attractive and vivacious lady, she bred Irish setters from a semi-detached house in North Baddesley near Romsey. She generally came to the surgery but I did do some house calls and I have never seen so many dogs in one house, plus the garden behind. Apart from her bedroom I suppose, every room seemed to contain them, but the house was clean, did not smell and they all looked well-fed and happy. I saw no sign of any Mr. Leavy or children, but she was always cheerful, paid her bills on time and was another of those clients whom I looked forward to seeing.

There is a serious disease in many breeds of dog, including Irish setters, called Hip Dysplasia (HD). This is where the 'ball' of the hip is either diminished or in the worst cases flattened, and the acetabulum (the socket into which healthy hips fit) is equally flattened or in bad cases non-existent. All careful breeders have their dogs radiographed and no affected cases are subsequently bred from. Indeed, there is an official register of dogs shown to be HD-free in all the breeds. Normally very prudent, Mrs. Leavy had bought Phoebe, a bitch puppy from another breeder in order to widen her genetic pool, which, it was claimed, came from HD-free stock. Alas it was not to be, and by the time Phoebe was six months old she was yelping in pain every time she moved her hind legs. I radiographed her and she had one of the worst cases of HD I had ever seen.

Nowadays full hip replacement surgery for dogs is available in such cases, but it was in its infancy then and we had a limited repertoire of surgical intervention techniques in practice. The most favoured was called 'Excision Arthroplasty' (EA), which is a fancy way of saying removal of the femoral head altogether. I had done several such ops, but never bilaterally at one sitting. It was felt that one hip joint, however bad, should support the other after a unilateral EA until it was healed, and then do the other one later. But Phoebe was in acute distress so, for the first and only time, I operated on both sides, one after the other.

It took her a while to recover, but she did very well. Within a month, false joints were forming and she was soon running around with good hind limb movement. Mrs. Leavy, as well as paying the fee (my first operation to date where I had charged over a hundred pounds, this being in 1978), also presented me with a solid silver 'hip' flask and I still have it. Phoebe was well homed-out to a caring owner but not bred from of course, and I spayed her before she went to her new abode.

Once, having advertised for a nursing position I was expecting a prospective candidate for interview and she arrived a little late and quite out of breath. She didn't explain why or make any fuss; the interview was fine and I was impressed by her but had some others in mind and at the end of it I told Maxine I would let her know. She looked disappointed. We walked out through the waiting area into the car park and I asked,

'Where's your car?'

'Ah well, that's the thing, and it's why I was late.'

'Yes?'

'Can you see that car up there on top of the hill?'

'The white one?'

'Yes, well it sort of blew up.'

'What?'

'I missed the entrance to the surgery and had just got to the top of that hill when the engine started making weird noises and then it went bang and died. It's very old. Then I looked down and could see your surgery so I ran.'

'Do you want me to drive you up to it?'

'No, don't worry, can I ring my boyfriend to come and get me?'

'Yes of course, and by the way, you've got the job.'

Calm in a crisis; one of the essential qualities. Veterinary nurses have a huge range of jobs to do in an average day and must be incredibly adaptable. As well as the pure nursing there is reception, advice to clients on the phone, giving appointments, taking fees, dealing courageously with aggressive or sometimes downright vicious animals, balancing anaesthesia, preparing all the instrument kits, sterilising, cleaning the practice and the theatre, being called by the vets to assist, accessing and filing record cards or running the computers; the list is endless.

I can't remember any nurse ringing in sick, though I did have occasionally to send one home who looked dreadful and shouldn't have struggled out of bed. Veterinary practices are the opposite of big human hospitals with their thousands of employees; the nurses knew instinctively that if they didn't get in to work a lot of it couldn't be done without them, and being a small practice there were never others around to replace them.

They never shirked, never complained about their work (well, not to me, anyway) and I have nothing but the highest admiration for them. Not one of them asked for a written contract though I always offered one, and all said more or less that if they were enjoying the work, I was happy with them and they were well paid, why bother with a contract? So, thank you Dawn, Sally, Moz, Jo, Maxine, Sarah, Debby, Tina, Alison one, Alison two, Anne, Lisa, Sue P; you were diamonds and the practice would not have known its success without you.

There was a large boys' public school just up the road called Embley Park and in the early days I had a succession of new clients who were teachers there, or their wives, giving it as their home addresses since most of the staff lived in. I got used to saying: 'Oh, you're a teacher up there, are you?' until a big rugby player-looking type came in and I asked the same question. 'No, I'm John King, the owner; I'm one of the idle rich,' which was modest of him as it was also a large estate with several farms and he ran it all. It had earlier been the home of the Nightingale family, with their daughter Florence.

His father was Jocelyn King who had been MP for Dorset South, and his mother the hilarious Hermione who became just about my favourite client. She had an adored poodle named Melody which, like many other poodles and indeed many breeds, had anal gland problems. These are small secretory glands - one on each side - just inside the anal sphincter. They don't have any real modern use and are referred to as 'vestigial glands'. In theory, as the motion is passed it squeezes the glands to empty their secretions onto it and give it a characteristic (revolting!) smell, as a 'mark-my-territory' idea. Yet marking territory in the modern context is useless and modern feeding often creates a rather sloppy poo, so they don't get squeezed properly and become engorged and uncomfortable. One of the clearest symptoms is 'scooting' the bottom along the ground (or worse, your Turkish carpet) in an attempt at relieving the itching.

So, vets up and down the country then and now, pull on a rubber glove and reluctantly empty them out, often several dogs per clinic. Another good reason for having extractor fans and deodorant sprays. Hermione roared with laughter once when I said, 'Come on then, let's get her up on the table and I can have a look at Hermione's bottom... oh dear... sorry... I mean Melody's.' Her husband the retired MP used to wait just outside the surgery door in his Rolls Royce Silver Shadow, which did my street cred no end of good.

The practice was blossoming and I had reached a point where as the only vet it was too high a workload. This often happens in single-handed practices or indeed any small-scale business. At some point, even though there probably isn't enough work for two full-time vets, you have to be courageous and expand. In the first six years I had employed several regular part-timers; two of them married lady vets who lived in the area and they were very good so long as they were just stand-ins for short periods and it was time for my first full-time vet assistant.

I was by then making plenty of money and had bought a pretty little cottage that needed restoration in the centre of town, on the Hundred. I got most of the building work done and just did some of the minor tasks myself when I had the time. My intention had been that it would be a house for the future assistant, as it was still common practice for a house and a car to be supplied with the job. In the event, he had bought a house where he had previously worked and when I took him on, he and his wife decided to sell that house and buy one in Romsey, so the cottage was not necessary for them. He moved on after a while and successfully put his plate up in nearby Salisbury.

He was followed by Celia Butler, who not only had the loveliest personality but was by far the best vet I ever employed. In all the years we worked together there was never a cross word or argument between us and I was very lucky to have found her. We had actually reached the point of starting to negotiate a partnership by her buying into the practice, but then she met Nick, who became her husband and she explained that as he worked for the Ordnance Survey there was some possibility that he would be promoted and have to leave the area. This didn't happen, but tragedy did. Soon after having their son George, Nick became very ill and was diagnosed with a completely incurable form of lymphoma and died at a distressingly young age. Celia bravely found baby care and continued working, and the last thing I heard from her was that she had married a widower with several children so I am very happy that George had brothers and sisters in the end.

It also freed me up to attend more veterinary evening meetings and at one such in Winchester, they were looking for a new secretary for the southern region of the BSAVA (British Small Animal Veterinary Association). My practice had originally been mostly LA but the SA side had grown rapidly and by that time it had ceased to be a mixed practice and was almost completely SA. I stood up at the meeting and said that I was rather young and had never done anything like that before but would willingly try. I was voted in (there weren't any other candidates) and for two years organised the local association as its secretary. We had monthly meetings around Hampshire, Wiltshire and the Isle of Wight and specialist guest speakers, chiefly from the universities.

One or other of the pharmaceutical companies was usually prepared to sponsor the evening as a PR exercise and provide food and coffee, as most members had shot straight out from their last appointments to get there in time. Then when the chairman resigned, I was promoted to that role and appointed a new secretary and that was a much easier job, just turning up for the meetings and presiding while the secretary did all the hard work.

There were also foreign congresses run from London by the main committees and one year I attended a BSAVA 'Congress in the Sun' in Torremolinos, Spain. Lectures were in the mornings before breakfast and evenings before dinner but between those we had time to look around the area, swim in the hotel pool and one day we took the ferry from nearby Algeciras to Morocco over the straits of Gibraltar and my first visit to Africa. On the plane on the way back I was chatting to the BSAVA President of that year, John Bower, whom I had met in Plymouth when I was a student, and asked him whether they had ever considered a 'Congress in the Snow'. Ever resourceful (and in those senior posts you soon get the hang of deputising) John said yes, it had been discussed by the executive committee but not yet acted upon, would I like to initiate and organise them? So I ran 'Congress in the Snow' for six years, mostly in Austria and Switzerland.

It was voluntary of course but since the travel companies routinely offered one free place per fifteen booked, with up to sixty attending I could get four free places to cover Dawn and I and the two university lecturers who had agreed to give the course. There were the travel and the hotels to book and also ensure that there were audio-visual facilities for the lectures. I soon learned not to take what the travel companies told me about lecture facilities as read. At the first congress - in Austria - the rep had said on the phone that there was a large bar area and they had a good projector and screen. We arrived to find a dim little bar, an ancient projector whose bulb promptly exploded and a dirty cream-coloured wall in a corner for projection. The hotel did not at all seem to see the importance of what we needed twice a day (despite my protestations in defective German) and I missed the first day's skiing by taking a bus down to Salzburg and buying three spare bulbs and a screen. In subsequent congresses, rather than relying on the travel firms I always contacted the hotels directly from the outset and we hit on an excellent one in Obergurgl, Switzerland which had everything we needed as well as an indoor pool and to which we returned each year.

I have mentioned the ten-year lease on my premises, and something rather unexpected happened. It was due to expire in three years and I had already started looking at options. I had no idea whether Whitbread would consider extending the lease and I had spotted one or two other premises for sale that might have done at a push. But on the day that I had gone to the solicitor's office to sign for the purchase of the cottage (not knowing that my future assistant would not need it), I got back to the practice and Sally said,

'Whitbread's have called, would you ring them back urgently?' It was Tony Barker.

'We've just had a major Board meeting and have now decided that we no longer have plans for your property. For accounting reasons we don't want to relinquish the freehold, but we can sell you a fifty-year lease. Are you interested?'

You bet I was interested and as the sitting tenant I also saw that I was in a strong negotiating position. We talked business and finally I persuaded them to make it ninety-nine years and at a subsequent meeting the price was agreed between us. But that was huge and I had just (ironically) spent my entire savings on the cottage. But it did get put to good use in the end and as in those days there was nothing that Midland Bank wouldn't do for me, we quickly negotiated a loan. Several years later and just before I finally sold the practice, Whitbread agreed to let me have the freehold for a modest sum and it made the ultimate sale in 1990 less complicated.

The locals in Romsey had often talked to me about how fond they had been of that large painting of the original 'Horse and Jockey' that was enclosed in a huge frame and as long as anyone could remember, had been hung on the high outside wall.

'The 'Orse and Jockey paintin', John, it was always there for us when we'd been off visiting places abroad like Salisbury, so we knew we wuz back in dear ol' Romsey when we saw it.' Being so enormous it had been the first thing you spotted as you drove down the hill towards the town from the west. Apart from the photo I had never seen it myself but tracked it down at a store in the Whitbread brewery. It was behind glass (the pane alone weighed about forty kg) and had been damaged by years outside in the rain, heat and frost but I made an offer and they sold it to me. I had it taken out of its frame, re-stretched and a bit of touching up done. Before the new extension was opened, I had it mounted up on a very high internal spine wall and it fitted perfectly. I got my loyal solicitors, Bells, to write a Covenant that since it had come 'home' it should remain where it was in perpetuity, and the locals (even non-pet owners) would often come in to admire it.

We were often asked whether we did 'dentistry' for animals and the answer was, 'well, yes… because someone has to do it,' and at that time there was no specialisation in that discipline. We couldn't do fillings, bridges, crowns or any advanced dentistry but just about every day there were 'dentals' to get done. Domestic animals do not often have caries; that is, holes being eaten away through the enamel which need filling, but their teeth frequently become dirty or encrusted with tartar as well as their roots becoming weak.

There were various brands of animal toothpastes for sale and some owners did manage to use them but it was usually only for the front teeth and it is never easy to persuade a dog or cat to 'open wide, please'. Almost all of the dentals were done under general anaesthesia and either extractions or 'scale and polish' were the normal procedures. For the latter we used a 'Cavitron'; an ultra-sound machine with various types of end probe that soon removed the tartar and had a water supply that washed away the debris. For ease of access and safety reasons, most animals were intubated to prevent water from entering the trachea.

A dentist client brought his dog in and asked if he could build him a crown for a missing molar so a few days later I anaesthetised the dog and watched with great interest. Another surgeon, this time a urogenital one, asked if he could attempt to remove his own dog's prostate gland which I had discovered was cancerous. It's easy to diagnose but a nightmare to operate on. Putting on one of those rubber gloves again, inside the rectum and about six centimetres along, it can be felt under the finger on the brim of the pelvis. To remove it was an operation far beyond my scope and, before the advent of fibre-optics it involved splitting the pubic symphysis for access and applying a retractor as the gland is deeply buried within the pelvic cavity.

Prostate enlargements ('hyperplasia') or tumours are very common in older male dogs and the routine treatment was heavy use of the synthetic female hormone oestradiol. Its side effects were predictable enough but it did give old dogs extra months or years to live. The surgeon said that the shape and anatomy of the canine prostate were not what he had expected and he was not sure that he had removed it all, but on heavy hormone therapy the dog lived anyway for two more years (even if he might have become rather unsure about his sexuality).

Chapter 4

Good clients, not-so-good clients

For a vet, 'clients' in general mean either farmers, horse owners or small animal (SA) owners. The latter have sometimes been parsed into 'companion animals' but I have left them as SA in this book. And they come in a fascinating array of shapes and sizes; as much a panoply as the variations in the whole of our human race. Some are angels, some are monsters; some are charming and reasonable, others aggressive and demanding. Some you look forward to seeing in your clinics, some you quietly wish would change to another practice and others just spoil your day. Just like GP doctors feeling the same about their patients, I suppose, but with one important distinction.

Unlike humans, a vet's patients don't behave in a way that threatens their well-being or survival and they never feign disease. The farm animals we see, the horses, dogs, cats, rabbits and all the others, instinctively govern their lives to survive as best as they can with the resources they have available. They do not smoke or drink themselves to death or refuse to take exercise or get into unnecessary conflict. Yes of course they may fight each other, whether dogs in the street, cats in back alleys or wild animals in the natural world. But in contrast to many humans, they basically seek to have the peace to live, eat and procreate, as the survival of their species demands.

In the SA sphere, it is the owners and clients that can unbalance this harmony in nature. It is they who decide how much they give their pets to eat and they who decide how much exercise they get. And that is extremely varied. I got a call from BBC TV South in Southampton who were running an evening current affairs item gleaned from one of the national dailies about how 'some owners come to resemble their pets'. The piece had referred to lugubrious, grumpy-looking male owners with bulldogs or perhaps tall, haughty and impeccably made-up ladies with Siamese cats. Could I come to the studio for an interview, bringing with me a 'well-padded' client, the producer asked on the phone, and their overweight dog? With a full list that day and three clinics I didn't have much time to prepare, so I warned my assistant that I would be away after 4 pm and rang the first client I could think of that fitted the description, saying that I would call at their house to whizz us in my car to the studios. Unfortunately, when I arrived at their house, they had decided to send their teenage daughter with me to appear with the obese black Labrador.

I had never been in a TV studio before, though I had done a weekend course run by the BSAVA about appearing on TV or in radio phone-ins. The main thing I retained from the course was, in the case of television, to get the presenter to tell you the first question they are going to ask. That should start you off in the strange and scary environment and help you to relax into subsequent questions. Everything seems so quiet and regulated when you see news broadcasts or current affairs programmes on TV and you could easily imagine that there's nobody much around, other than the presenter and a few cameras.

The truth is that everything behind is full of activity and only goes silent when on air. You walk in with a producer, stepping over cables, squeezing past people with clipboards and trying to ignore the ribald conversations between cameramen. There is the banter between the floor manager and the producers, the quips of technicians and generally it's an unexpectedly frenetic environment. On the radio side, my main recollection of the course was the advice to try to 'modulate your voice up and down as much as you possibly can', even to the point of exaggeration, because nothing sounds worse over the radio waves than a dull, monotonous voice. With this in mind, I did my best to combine the two and the interview went surprisingly well considering it was my first on TV, though I had done some phone-ins. With obesity already having started its meteoric rise I had a chance to talk on national television about exercise and correct feeding although I did, after the event, feel sorry for the daughter who was a last-minute stand-in and only slightly overweight.

The 'obesity' consultation often went a bit like this:

'How much does he have to eat altogether in a day?'

'Well, just his breakfast - dog biscuits - and then his tinned food in the evening.'

'Nothing in between?'

'I do give him a few shortbreads when I'm having my morning coffee.'

'Anything else?'

'Well, my husband is very naughty and he will give him bits when we have our lunch. I've told him about it.'

'Anything during the afternoon?'

'Yes, but just a few treats.'

'Any chocolate?'

'The children sometimes give him some. I've told them not to.'

'About how much food does he have in the evening?'

'Oh, just a tin.'

'A seven-ounce tin?'

'No, one of those bigger ones.'

I would do a quick calculation and often find that the dog was getting approximately twice the calorie intake it needed in a day and even more for the really lazy ones. So, it was generally goodbye to all the treats and the owners were under orders dramatically to increase their pets' exercise, halve the tinned food, bulk it out by adding plain bran to it, that contains almost no calories but fills their stomach, or use prescription low-calorie diets.

Most clients, when initially giving their names for the record cards, were happy to be put down as 'Mr.' or 'Mrs.'; some preferred their title such as 'Dr.' which was fine, but others were more pushy. There were some army barracks not far away and although the officers themselves were generally quite decent and modest about their ranks, it was their wives who were not.

'Your name?'

'Captain Morris.'

'That's your name.'

'No, it's my husband's.'

'Will he be bringing the cat here?'

'No, it will always be me; does it matter?'

'It's just for the record.'

'Well get on with it, then.'

I overheard that particular exchange and caught Alison's muttered aside, 'You'll be the Captainess, then.' It did matter in a way because when that record card got filed away for the next time, it risked going in under the 'Cs' rather than under the correct surname and once misfiled they were a swine to relocate. Of course, it's all so much easier now with computer records (unless the whole system goes down and then you can't find any case notes at all, rather than just losing the odd one).

But other clients were much more modest. A tall, quietly-spoken, very patrician gentleman came in for an appointment whom I suppose gave his name as 'Mr. Hodgkinson'. It was in November and his dog was quite poorly, so I saw him frequently and any number of times must have walked into the waiting room with his record card in my hand, 'Mr. Hodgkinson, please.' We got the dog better in time for the festive season and I received a Christmas card warmly thanking me for everything I had done, from Air Chief Marshall Sir Derek Hodgkinson. Sort of says it all, doesn't it?

My nurses were always very patient with difficult clients and seldom complained to me about them (though I know they shared plenty of wicked jokes at their cost between themselves), but there was another – retired - army captain whom they always said was obnoxious to them. Still brandishing his rank, he would be obsequious on the phone, patronising and belittling towards them when he arrived and, they said, was constantly looking at other parts of their bodies than their faces. After the second complaint he seemed quite shocked when I gave him his record cards and told him to find another vet. I think he had assumed that as my practice was also a business, I wouldn't dream of refusing his clientèle. That evening the nurses took me out for a drink.

A new client came in carrying a black cat in a basket in a terrible condition; emaciated, covered in fleas and with several open bite abscesses.

'I'm a single man and Blackie has always been a big part of my life. But he disappeared three months ago. I looked everywhere and put adverts in the newsagents and local paper, but nothing. And then yesterday evening he just turned up. He hopped in through his cat door and looked for his bowl. But you can see the condition he's in.'

'Well, we'll sort out the abscesses, de-flea him and then you can feed him up.'

'It's a miracle really, he went straight upstairs after I'd fed him and went to sleep on the bed he's always had, in my spare room.'

'One thing we'll also have to do is castrate him, as that's probably why he went off.'

'No, he's already been done, I took him to my previous vet when he was six months old.'

'Let me check... no... he certainly hasn't been neutered.'

'But that's impossible... or can they grow back?'

'No, they can't. There seems to be only one possibility here; he isn't your cat.'

'But it really is Blackie. He knew me immediately, miaowed, circled around my legs as he always did and he knew where everything was.'

'Well, it's a double miracle then. He obviously loves you and he's yours, isn't he?'

An attractive young couple brought in their recently-acquired female kitten for vaccination. We were a nurse short that day and I was filling in the client record card myself.

'And what's her name?' I asked.

'Er... do we have to tell you?' the young woman blushed.

'Well, it's just to know what to call her, really.'

'She's called... "Boobs".'

Good clients, not-so-good clients

. . .

It was always fun to meet interesting new owners, and almost the next clients also brought kittens, this time males. They had named them 'Castor' and 'Pollux' after the twin sons of Leda, and these two had really done their homework. According to Homer, they recounted (and this was in the days when you got things out of books rather than cut and paste them out of Wikipedia), the boys were not true twins. They were the result of a sort of double fertilization between their mortal father and crafty old Zeus, King of the Gods and always on the lookout for new virgins. He had temporarily transformed Leda into a swan and she laid two eggs, each containing twins. One bore Clytemnestra (who married Agamemnon) plus Castor and the other brought Pollux and his true twin, Helen, who later became Helen of Troy. I then managed to lower the intellectual tone of the conversation by remarking that if Castor got lost one evening and they were roaming the streets shouting 'Castor! Castor!', that would be all right, but maybe not 'Pollux'.

The clinic was immediately opposite the 5000-acre Broadlands Estate, the home of Earl Mountbatten and his family. I was aware that his farm work was done by one of the bigger practices but I wondered who looked after his domestic pets. My question was answered one lunchtime when two harassed-looking footmen rushed into the practice saying, 'Come quickly, his Lordship's dog is having fits.' I grabbed some primidone (the usual treatment for epilepsy) and my case and followed their car through the gates into the estate, ran up the steps of the main entrance and into the lift up to the Earl's bedroom, where his black Labrador was lying on the carpet. But these weren't epileptic fits; these were full-on convulsions and every nine or ten seconds he was being wracked with tetanic contractions that squeeze the life out of the heart and lungs.

He was close to death and I was trying, in the seconds available, to scroll down in my mind to Professor Holmes' toxicology lectures at Langford. I arrived at the rapid conclusion that the only substance that could cause those symptoms in an otherwise healthy dog (remember that I had never seen him before, let alone been in the bedroom of the Queen's uncle) was the poison, strychnine.

But strychnine was illegal in Britain and I'd never seen a case of it; how on earth could he have got hold of it? There is no specific antidote and the only hope is to deeply anaesthetise the animal, where finding a vein, without a nurse and in a dog shuddering with convulsions was a tall order. Luckily, I had a bottle of Sagatal in my case (pentobarbitone); the footman did exactly what I told him to, I got a vein on the second attempt and injected an entirely uncalculated amount into his blood. There had been no time to weigh him and compute the right dose so it was complete guesswork, but he was dying and I had seconds.

After the injection, he seemed at first to relax but then had another huge convulsion; his mucous membrane colour went purple-black and I thought 'It's too late'. Then he just lay there, not breathing. Damn. Either the convulsions or the Sagatal has killed him ... nothing ... but then ... a little breath ... just a tiny one, followed by a second, stronger and then a more normal one. Then he was breathing calmly and the convulsions were temporarily over.

We rushed him into my car, drove him back to the clinic and put him onto intensive care, which gave me a chance to look up a toxicology textbook to check what the half-life of strychnine was as it was slowly metabolised away. If we could keep him under for long enough, he should survive. In the end he remained completely anaesthetised for two days; each time as it was wearing off, the shudders returned, but then on the third day he woke up and was fine, if shocked.

Earl Mountbatten's gamekeepers denied it to the end, but it seemed that strychnine had been obtained illegally and they had (so the rumour went) been baiting rabbit paunches to leave out to kill foxes that had been attacking baby pheasants destined for the shoot. It even got back to me later that the head keeper had alleged – unbelievably - that it was my treatment that had caused the convulsions, but of course he was in danger of losing his job.

The Earl, in writing to thank me a few weeks later, asked if the dog would be well enough to take with him to Classiebawn in Ireland, his family home there. I felt that he would need a bit more recovery time and so the dog stayed behind at Broadlands. And that was a few days before it happened; the horrifying murder of the Earl by the IRA while on a fishing trip, together with his grandson Nicholas, a young friend of his and the mother of his son-in-law. Four died on that dreadful day, his daughter Lady Pamela and her husband Lord Brabourne were terribly injured and remained in wheelchairs for years after, and Nicholas's twin brother was initially blinded. The country, and Romsey in particular to whom he had been such a friend and patron, were in shock and mourning. The entire Royal family came to the funeral and his body lies in Romsey Abbey, as he had requested in his will.

Things returned very slowly to normal, as they must in human life, and Broadlands was passed to his grandson Norton, the elder brother of poor Nicholas who died. Lord Mountbatten and his wife Lady Edwina had no sons, only their daughter Pamela who had become Lady Brabourne, so Norton took the title Lord Romsey during his mother's life, with the right to later become the new Earl Mountbatten. He and his delightful wife Lady Penelope became clients of the practice and they subsequently agreed to officially open a large new extension I was having built at the time. Although the property was listed, I succeeded in getting planning consent to enlarge it externally and this doubled the size of the practice.

I was sad in the end to sell the practice but by that time in the early 1990s, I was becoming deeply involved with the University of Southampton and my future life. Romsey always was a sweet little town with kind, happy people and on a return trip I saw that although it has grown substantially, it still retains that pleasant small-town quality, with lots of independent shops and a thriving town centre. The few eyesores from my time there had been removed, the new-builds are spot on and congratulations to the planners, architects and no doubt local opinion, for having succeeded in enlarging it without losing its old-fashioned charm.

This gave me the chance to have a look at a lot of other veterinary practices in the UK and elsewhere while I did locums during the university vacations.

CHAPTER 5

GOOD PRACTICES, NOT-SO-GOOD PRACTICES

Life is a rich tapestry and in all walks of it there are the good and there are the bad. There are good vets, doctors, teachers, architects and bad ones. Most of us are neither completely one or the other and hope only to be reasonably competent; in general practice, you are a jack of all trades and master of none. It had been endlessly debated within the profession whether specialisation should take place at the level of the vet schools; the subject is so vast, the textbooks so numerous and the five or six years in which you study really not enough to handle more than a fraction of the knowledge that is out there. And vets must learn about all the common species too.

In some areas, things are similar between species but in most they are completely different and I remember feeling slightly jealous of med student friends at Bristol who only had to learn the intricate details of one species; humans. The debate always seemed to end with the same conclusion; vets should continue to be trained in all the species and all the branches of medicine and surgery that involve them. Of course, working with just one or two species has become the norm after you qualify and there are less and less of the 'general workmen' like me who could turn their hand to anything, even if it justifies the criticism that we don't do any of it particularly well.

You might get away with it if you are a dentist, physio or private consultant, but as a vet you can't shut your surgery for a week or two if you need a holiday. You must find a 'locum', that is, someone to cover for you; the word locum being short for 'locum tenens', Latin for 'taking the place'. In my early days, to get a weekend off or a holiday I employed quite a few. As you will read in the chapter 'Bureaucracy', the RCVS insisted that all practices maintain emergency cover twenty-four hours a day including weekends, and as I was single-handed for the first five years of the practice, the occasional locums were a godsend. But that did not mean that they were all good and, once again, they came in all shapes and sizes.

I was expecting an Australian one before getting away for a week in Crete and, exhausted and grumpy one Sunday afternoon – and looking forward to my first spell off call for three months – this tall, leather-clad biker strode into my garden. I shouted at him that it was 'Private Property!' He took off his helmet, put out his hand and said, 'Hi, I'm Linsay, the locum,' and I remember thinking, 'Did he come all the way from there on his bike?' Of course, he was doing what a lot of recently-qualified Aussie, New Zealander or South African vets did; fly over, buy some transport, get lucrative locum jobs around UK and tour at the same time. He turned out to be very competent and being also young and good-looking, the nurses thought he was lush. In fact, they were bitterly disappointed when the old boss arrived back and he had to move on. Just after, I spotted on a record card that he had forgotten the word for 'constipated' and had written 'Can't go to the dunny'; beautifully Australian.

But there were some poor ones too, and after another such week one of the nurses rushed at me the morning I got back, threw her arms around me and spluttered, 'Thank God you're back, he was terrible! Nothing has actually died but that was mostly thanks to us.' I took them out to dinner on that news. In fact, I had already recognised him when he arrived in Romsey. He was that awful lecturer in pig medicine that we had had at Langford, so it turned out that he was as bad at locums as he had been as a teacher. But when you've booked a rare holiday it's too late of course, and I had to hope that with the guidance of my expert nurses, he wouldn't make a pig's ear of it if you'll excuse the pun.

Another locum I employed just once was a young vet whom I knew a little, as his parents lived nearby. He was very presentable, well-spoken and newly qualified from my old alma mater so I thought I'd give him a try, but I didn't know he was fanatically religious. The nurses told me that whether he was consulting or operating he always had a Bible open near to him, and would actually interrupt operations for a few seconds to walk over to it and read a piece of text, asking them to turn the pages as he was scrubbed up. But no dramas or catastrophes happened while he was there, so 'God moved in a mysterious way', I suppose.

For occasional weekends after doing Saturday morning surgery, I employed husband and wife Margaret and Arthur Baskerville. They were both vets, but she had spent most of her time since qualifying raising their young family and he was an R&D pathologist at a local research establishment, where animal testing was known to be taking place. So, although neither of them was experienced in general work they functioned well as a team; I trusted them and they gave me the odd weekend.

The vexed question of animal testing is not one that I have the space or even the knowledge to discuss fully in these pages; there are strong arguments in favour of it and equally strong ones against. Most new drugs, whether destined for veterinary or human use (or as commonly, both), before coming onto the market need to be shown to be safe and effective and the correct doses established, and at the time this was normally done by testing on laboratory animals.

Just as one example, if the dangerous drug thalidomide, used against morning sickness in women had been tested on pregnant animals, a different drug might have been used, and the tragedy of the thousands of children subsequently born with severe malformations averted. It is obvious that animal testing should be ended if other equally effective methods could be found to protect human beings, but until a perfect system is found, it is a necessary evil. Others did not take that view and in the 1980s and 90s there were fanatics, some becoming known as the 'Animal Rights' or 'Animal Liberation' groups, of varying levels of militancy, from peaceful protests and lobbying of MPs to violently breaking into laboratories, opening the cages, releasing the test animals and worse.

Nobody would argue that these poor creatures had a wonderful life and many had to be sacrificed at the end for pathology reports. But at the top of the chain, it was human health and life that was at stake. Researchers had already started doing, wherever possible, 'non-sacrificial' trials, where animals such as beagle dogs were tested with, for example, new vaccines, but with only blood samples taken and observation for side effects and the aim of re-homing them afterwards.

Good Practices, Not-so-good Practices

One single example of a huge subject was where an entirely new virus called parvovirus entered the country and litters of plump, healthy pups were reduced within days to dehydrated skeletons passing blood until they died. Being a virus, no real treatment was available though all vets tried to maintain life with fluid therapy in the hope that they might produce antibodies and get through it. But later a vaccine was developed and was in the advanced stages of testing, on beagles in a sterile environment. This was necessary to establish that the vaccine was producing the correct antibodies without stray viruses or bacteria impeding the test. One animal rights group broke into the lab, took some of the dogs home and released the rest outside. They had been removed from the controlled environment, the results were invalidated and the protocol had to be re-started from scratch. Vets had to wait an extra four months for the vaccine and in the meanwhile many young animals died.

A violently obsessed group of these militants had targeted (what they thought was) Arthur's car outside their home near Salisbury and had attached a bomb underneath it, timed to explode during his journey to work. But in the event, they had mistaken it for Margaret's car and she left in it to do a much shorter trip. Mercifully it exploded just after she got out of it and she survived with bruising and shock.

When I started doing locums myself, most of the practices were excellent, but some not so good. Arriving at one in London I was surprised to see notices posted around the practice concerning economy; either with disposable syringe use, vaccine administration, which antibiotics to use and avoid, and the like. It is true that for economy some practices including my own used to, for example, sterilise and recycle some of the syringes and needles in good condition (though not for intravenous work) and while strictly speaking it was discouraged, it did at least lead to re-cycling of plastic and metals and in many ways, it was acceptable so long as they were sharp and autoclaved. But it was rare to see instructions to use what may be inferior treatment.

At that practice I also observed something that I hadn't seen since the sixties; animals routinely induced for anaesthesia with the volatile liquid, ether. It has the advantage that it is relatively safe in an anaesthetic sense and very cheap, but the downside is that when mixed with oxygen it's a stinging, acrid gas and very upsetting for the patients involved. Cats needed to be held by one operator with the front and back legs held tightly in each hand and another person to hold the mask on and they struggled and screeched until it kicked in. But, like chloroform, it had been supplanted by much more humane induction agents, notably thiopentone for dogs (with fluothane gas added once unconscious) and Saffan for cats. Both are given intravenously as they only work that way, or a new generation of anaesthetic agents that can now be given intramuscularly or even subcutaneously (under the skin).

To see cats being 'masked down' as it was called then shocked me and even more so because ether is explosive; the boss smoked heavily and I saw him more than once near the theatre carrying a lighted cigarette. My attention was also drawn to a price list in the dispensary where again, each was given in order of price and we were required, whenever possible, to use the cheapest. There's nothing wrong with economy, and in my own practice we had always tried to combine that with effectiveness, but when an outdated and unpleasant substance is no longer necessary it seems churlish to continue to use it.

I was beginning to see many other truths about this practice, supplemented by tales from the nurses, who had rather befriended me. I had been there about a week and the crunch came during one morning surgery. A very nice lady came in with a seven-month-old female cat in a lot of pain.

'I usually go to the Blue Cross where I can get free veterinary treatment but they won't see more than two animals per family and this kitten, which makes three, was foisted on me by my children.' She seemed to have a nasty 'greenstick' fracture (where the soft young bone bends a little, rather than breaking) of the femur, but she was in such a lot of distress that it was impossible to touch the area.

'We need to X-ray her,' I advised the client.

'Will it cost a lot?'

'Well, quite a bit, yes.'

'The thing is I have very little money but I've got a tenner with me and can pay a little every week, that I promise.' She seemed very genuine and I went into reception, looked at the appointments book and saw that I had a ten-minute gap immediately after her.

'Has she eaten?'

'No, she doesn't want to.'

'I'm not surprised. Look, I'm going to give her a very short-acting anaesthetic here and now and we'll radiograph her. That will be the cheapest for you.'

With domestic animals almost all radiography needs to be done anaesthetised, for a number of reasons. Firstly, few animals can be persuaded to lie motionless on a radiograph cassette or not jump when the noise of the exposure-timer disturbs them. Any such radiograph will probably be blurred and useless. Secondly, it is to protect the operators - almost always the nurses - because otherwise they would have to hold the animals and be exposed to the X-rays directly. These are highly dangerous and multiple exposures can lead to tissue damage; even leukaemia and other forms of cancer. I quickly knocked out the little puss with a tiny dose of thiopentone, took a rapid picture and processed it in the darkroom myself while the client waited. I showed her the radiograph; it was a true greenstick fracture (they are very painful but don't need support) and she woke up quickly.

'There's very little we can do about the pain' (cats poorly tolerate analgesics such as aspirin or opiates) 'but it will get less each day and within a week she should be much better.'

'Thank you so much. What do I owe?'

'Let's call it twenty pounds.' (This was in 1990).

'Thank you. I'll pay ten now and bring in five pounds twice in the next two weeks.'

At lunchtime, the boss called me to his smoke-filled office.

'What's all this about the greenstick fracture?' I explained the situation to him.

'But all animals must be admitted for the day for that sort of procedure,' he barked.

'Why?'

'Well, for one thing, for it to be done properly and for another, to be charged correctly. I understand you only asked her for twenty pounds.'

'That's right.'

'Are you determined to do everything contrary to the rules of this practice?'

'I thought it was the right thing to do in her case.'

'Well, we're not a charity for single mothers who can't afford their fees.'

That was it. I saw red and told him there and then what I thought of some of the things I'd observed in his rotten practice. He dismissed me on the spot and told me I'd be paid until the previous day. I was putting some stuff into my car at the back of the practice preparing to leave when two of the nurses rushed out in tears.

'We can't believe you've been sacked; you were like a breath of fresh air here.' They were exaggerating but it was sweet of them to have said it.

Through a locum agency, the next job I got was at a SA practice near Manchester, for two weeks. On paper, and according to the agency, it was a good practice, with a main clinic and a branch some distance away and another vet was responsible for that branch. I had had no personal contact with the practice owner before I arrived but had explained to the agency that I was a keen runner and believed in eating healthily. Could my accommodation be some sort of house or flat with a kitchen – even a tiny one - where I could cook for myself? The agency confirmed that as the owner was going on holiday to Spain I would be staying at her own house and could share the kitchen with her sister, who also lived there. I would be given a phone and there was a practice car which would be supplied. That was a relief as by that time I was living in France and driving a very wacky old 2CV repainted to look like a brick wall which would not look good arriving at house calls.

I came off the ferry, stayed at a friend's flat in Southampton on the Saturday night and on Sunday drove north. I arrived at her house – well, a house in the country following a map that I had been emailed before the days of

SatNav - to find it apparently empty; at least no one opened the door. There was also no name by the bell. I sat and waited for an hour and the boss eventually arrived – I was relieved that I was actually at the right house - and she remarked that she had forgotten to leave a note on the door, without actually apologising.

She then renegued on every detail that had been agreed with the agency. Her sister had changed her mind and did not want to share the house and she had booked me into a small hotel, miles from the main practice, in fact one exit down the motorway. 'But it's OK, it's got a microwave!' she shrilled. Whoopee. I would be eating warmed-up processed food for a fortnight. The practice Ford was still in the garage, she said, so I'd have to use my own car. The 'practice phone' was, unbelievably, a battered old pager (or 'bleeper') and then, the icing on the cake:

'Do my nights on call start tomorrow or Tuesday?'

'You're doing every night.'

'Every day and every night for two weeks?'

'My assistant's husband is also a vet but he works for another practice. They have a young family and can't be called out simultaneously.'

'So, I'm on for... let me see... well, several hundred hours including nights with no free time at all?'

'Yes, and my son Dragan is practice manager and he'll be keeping an eye on you.'

If I hadn't travelled all that way for the job I would have turned around, got back into the 2CV and told her to stuff her job. I was very close to it, but I had bought the return ferry tickets, wanted to keep up with new professional developments and we needed the money, so I bit my tongue and accepted it. The hotel turned out to be an unmanned one and she had given me the front door passcode and a keycard for my room. There was a microwave

Good practices, not-so-good practices

but no kettle and, it being a Sunday evening and no shops around, my dinner that night was some chocolate I had bought on the boat and the next morning's breakfast a cup of tap water before I could get some supplies. By the end of two weeks of mostly eating vitamin-free rubbish I didn't have the energy to go for even the briefest jog before work in the mornings.

With my first night duty starting on Monday, I asked the nurses that afternoon how the pager worked.

'If it bleeps, you'll see a telephone number scrolling across the screen.'

'What do I do then?'

'You ring that number.'

'But there isn't a phone in my hotel, I've checked.'

'Er... I don't know... you'll have to find a telephone box.'

'Any idea where the nearest one is?'

'No, I don't live down there.'

'I've got my own mobile here, it's French but I'll try it.'

I didn't get a bleep that evening thankfully and did try the mobile from the hotel but it didn't connect. I also experimented with the UK 0044 prefix as the 'roving' system for foreign calls was not yet well established, but that didn't work either. So I went out for a walk and found a small park with a telephone box.

For my younger readership – all with smartphones - let me explain how things worked in the Middle Ages. If you didn't have a fixed phone at home you went to something called a telephone box, a bit like a red Tardis. There you put some coins into a slot and dialled the number you wanted. If it was answered, you pressed the 'A' button and could speak to whom you called. If it wasn't answered, you pressed the 'B' button and got your money back. Then later, in most phone boxes until they were abandoned altogether, you didn't use coins but a BT telephone card, bought at the post office or a tobacconist. I checked the one at the park and it was the card version, so the next day at lunchtime went and bought one (not reimbursed by the practice). They are almost extinct now, though recently we did find one sweet old-fashioned coin-operated telephone box in Portwrinkle, Cornwall, still in working order.

I got my first bleep on the third evening, wrote down the number and jogged over to find the phone box in use. But, tantalizingly, quite a few teenagers seemed to be sitting around on the adjacent benches, looking bored and saying on their phones, 'What'ya doin'... naa not much... yeah... ok... laters.' I couldn't help smiling grimly to myself that I was a middle-aged locum vet on call, waiting to get back to an animal owner about something apparently very urgent, while these young folk had mobiles but didn't have anything to say to their mates while I stood around.

I even considered giving one of them a few pound coins and asking if I could use their phone, but then imagined the flashing blue light outside my ground-floor hotel room when one of the parents had reported me for trying to press money onto minors. I probably only got half a dozen out-of-hours calls in the two weeks I was there and it worked all right except when it rang when I was asleep. Then I had to get the light on, grab my pen and scribble down the number before it finished. Equally, for arriving at the unlit telephone box in the dark I had needed to buy a torch to see the details I had just written down. And remember this wasn't all that long ago; so much has changed.

One night I got a weird number, not starting with a zero and not really looking like a phone number at all. But I wasn't familiar with the local codes and assumed that some numbers may not need one. It was about midnight. I ran to the phone box and called the number.

'Yeah, what?'

'Hello, it's the vet, you rang about an emergency.'

'No, I didn't.'

'Is your number…?' I gave it to him.

'No, it isn't; look, is this a wind-up?'

'Not at all, there's been a mistake, I'm sorry.'

'You'd better be, I have to get up at five.'

I rang the call-minding centre that sent out the bleeps.

'Hello it's Mr. Sampson the vet, has there just been a call for me?'

'Let's see… no, nothing for you since 8.24 this evening, did you get that one?'

'Yes, I dealt with that but I've just had another.' I gave him the number I had rung.

'No, certainly not from us; it doesn't sound to me like a phone number at all.'

The next morning, I asked the nurses and showed them the pager. They explained to me at last how to access past messages by pressing on a button I hadn't previously spotted and they saw that weird number.

'Oh, it's the winning lottery numbers. Dragan sometimes uses that pager and he likes to get them sent through.' This was my first skirmish with the famous 'practice manager' whom after four days I had not yet had the dubious pleasure of meeting.

However, it was not all bad and the other vet turned out to be lovely, invited me once to dinner (home-cooked food with vegetables, yummy), generally took pity on me and she did two of the nights to at least give me a bit of breathing space. The old Ford arrived at the practice, dropped off by the garage and apparently repaired but covered in filth, so I washed it and drove it back to my room down the motorway that evening. But it wouldn't start the next morning so I had to hitch-hike back up the motorway and, sprinting, arrived late for the first clinic. One of the nurses was off sick and we were struggling through surgery, when the remaining one said,

'I'm going to have to lock the practice.'

'Why?'

'The boss has rung from Spain that she hasn't got enough cash and I've got to go to the bank and arrange a transfer.'

'No need to lock up, I'll mind the place and man the phones while you're away.'

'No, she says she wants it locked.'

'With me inside?'

'No, with you outside.' She didn't even trust me to be alone in the practice. By that time, I really had begun to think I was working for a fruit loop. It seems she had been married to a Croatian, and Dragan was the result. For a 'practice manager', his complete absence was a bit of a mystery but at length a cocky nineteen-year-old in torn jeans and a backward-facing baseball cap wandered in as I was finishing the ops.

'You lookin' after my mum's practice OK?'

'Yes, I hope so.'

'You checkin' the drugs and vaccine stocks?'

'Am I supposed to?'

'Yeah, cos we don't like to get overstocked, messes up the cash flow.'

'I leave that to the nurses, but anything I want I'll tell them to order.'

'Yeah, just not too much, OK?'

'Understood.'

'Cos I'm busy with all the bankin' and appointments with the accountant an'that.'

I'll stop the transcription of that conversation there before you lose the will to live. The next day we had a series of operations needing intravenous fluids and when a dehydration case came in, I said to the nurse, 'Number nineteen and a giving set, please.' She looked at me imploringly,

'There are no more giving sets left.'

'What! Why?'

'Because we're not allowed to have more than six in stock.'

'Dragan, I suppose, but we have to give this dog fluids.'

'We can order more here for tomorrow.'

'That doesn't help this dog, does it?'

In the event we had to, completely against all the rules of sterility, resort to a clean but used one. That was unprofessional on my part but the dog improved and by the next day there were fifteen giving sets in the cupboard - they don't even cost much. And it was no real surprise, after he gave me my cheque on the final Sunday before I left for France, that it bounced. The second one went through, though, after a stinking letter.

Veterinary practice managers are a mixed breed; I have met some excellent ones and others quite useless, such as the spoilt brat above. In his case, he wasn't a practice manager at all; the nurses detested him and told me of his constant posturing, saying how important he was and ordering them around but still getting up at midday. Larger practices do need a proper manager, however, although that role is sometimes best filled by a long-serving receptionist or secretary, and indeed the three best ones I met had been one of those. They knew the practice inside out, recognised most clients by the sound of their voices on the phone and respected the skilled work of the nurses; others had previously been nurses themselves.

The worst two I encountered were at clinics where in one case the (unemployed) husband of the boss took the role and in the other, it was the practice principal's wife. Both turned out to be disastrous; stroppy, arrogant, disdainful of the nurses and incompetent. Once when I advertised for a nurse, three of them from the same practice applied, each saying that they couldn't bear the new manager and none of them knew that the others had come for interview. On the reverse side of the coin, at one other large practice where I did a locum in Kent, the practice principal had decided to do much less vet work himself and became the manager, very successfully.

I only ever met one human hospital administrator and that was under extreme circumstances. I had had an argument with an exploding mole trap and lost; it was on a workbench and a piece of the charge flew directly into my right eye. I was operated on as an emergency at midnight in a heroic attempt at saving the sight of that eye. The next morning I was lying in my hospital bed feeling very shocked when an administrator came into my room and asked if he could put some questions to me. I replied that I really didn't feel well enough, but he persisted. It was only when I realized that I couldn't possibly answer his questions about the 'hospital experience' and the food, staff, services and so on that I politely asked him to leave. He said he would come back when I felt better but he didn't. Since then, there has been quite an uproar about hospital management, including the following article in *The Week* (24.12.2022, p6):

'An NHS Trust has been widely mocked for advertising for a "director for lived experience" on a salary of £110,000 p.a. The ad, posted by the Midlands Partnership Foundation Trust, says the "exciting new post" – reportedly a first in the NHS – required someone who is "interpersonally talented" and a "strategic bridge-builder". Candidates should have "personal experience of life-altering health conditions and power imbalances."'

No wonder doctors and nurses, doing real jobs with real patients on the front line, are so incensed by job ads like these. As a comparison, I'm convinced I'm right in claiming that there is no veterinary practice manager who works from a different building such as an 'administration block' and is only occasionally seen at the cutting edge. They are always around and, crucially, should be an essential part of the team. They see the full waiting room, the op lists, the kennels packed with animals being observed, treated or waiting for/recovering from surgery, while the vets rush around trying to keep up. Even in my small practice there were days when unexpected emergencies meant that I hadn't even started the ops list when the owners were already booked to collect their animals to take home a few hours later. And you may say, 'Yes, but there must be less popular, quieter practices.' And you'd be right, but they don't need a manager. The vets, nurses and staff in those have enough downtime to run the practice efficiently themselves.

I have personally known doctors and nurses driven to exhausted tears by the avalanche of directives, targets, spreadsheets, instructions and even blackmail from people in remote admin departments who know very little about medicine or surgery. If I were an architect asked to design a brand-new hospital there would be no administration block. Every major ward would have an office for the manager to get on with the essential job of running all of its aspects; rotas, replacement of absent staff, liaising with suppliers, catering, laundry, porterage and all the other important jobs that keep an efficient department going. They would also deal with complaints. How much more insight an administrator would have if an aggrieved patient or ex-patient complained about a certain junior doctor making a mistake, if they knew first-hand that that young doctor had just been finishing a double shift? Whereas a complaint received over at the admin block would far more likely be referred menacingly back to the doctor involved and even their registration threatened. Nobody who does an eight-hour shift in daylight and no weekends could understand what junior medical staff have to go through. And although in a previous chapter, I have mentioned being mildly bullied as a young vet, there is otherwise no comparison. A doctor I knew was a senior registrar in emergency medicine and had a message from administration that a junior manager would be shadowing her through one night shift in A&E as a 'time and motion' initiative. The young lady turned up at 7 pm having apparently been given the day off, followed her around until 10 pm expressing regular distaste at the sort of things she was seeing and then announced that she was going home as she 'needed her sleep.'

There would need to be one or two 'Supremos' somewhere in the hospital who coordinated them all and took the bigger decisions but they would not be above discipline, and if poor they could be replaced. Doctors, nurses and all the front line would AT LAST be valued and encouraged in their mission to get patients better and back home as soon as possible, and billions could be saved. When the running and control of hospitals is returned to the medical staff who know what they are doing and taken away from ambitious politicians and lazy bureaucrats, sanity will be returned.

Now, would someone help me down from this pulpit, please? I'm 75 and my legs aren't what they were. I know I'm just a vet and couldn't possibly understand the complexities of a huge hospital, but we do know how to run a medico-surgical business efficiently, without wastage of time or effort, to get the work done, balance the books and avoid useless bureaucracy. Well, most of it, anyway. I'll return to this controversial area in Chapter Eight.

I also did locums in excellent clinics, I am happy to report. In one in Sussex, I was replacing the assistant who told me the story of her chaotic road accident. She and her boyfriend lived in deepest countryside on a long, straight, unlit, usually deserted road. Their black retriever occasionally ran out of the door and would cross the main road to the other side but would then normally come back immediately to their calls. That winter evening, they shouted for him but he was nowhere to be seen. They saw car headlights appearing fast in the distance and as the car got nearer the dog appeared on the other side of the road. They shouted 'Stay!!' but he started to cross the road towards them.

She ran into the road, grabbed him and waved her arm at the lights, but the car had not seen her, the side of its bumper hit her hard and it came to rest thirty metres further up. She was down on the tarmac having broken her leg, could not move and had let go of the dog who ran away again, but then headlights appeared from the OTHER direction. Her boyfriend ran into the road waving and shouting, fearing that she would be run over twice, the driver emergency braked but hit and injured the dog and just managed to stop in front of him.

The assistant had a bad tibial fracture with terrible bruising and, fearing 'compartment syndrome', which is a common complication of tibial fractures, it was decided to plaster her rather than plating. As I was leaving the practice two weeks later, she was still in a great deal of pain and said that she could feel the fracture moving slightly under the plaster, but I rang later and she reported that it was healing after further treatment.

And some practices are 'not-so-good' in a 'good' way; that is, when they take on work with the best of intentions but are just not up to scratch or are attempting work that is too specialised. I had a great deal of sympathy with that position because, after all, if you are not ambitious and only stick pedantically to the things you know you can do easily, how do you improve or develop?

I can certainly admit in my own practice to sometimes having taken on 'tricky' cases that might have been better passed on to an expert; it's a very fine line and can only be assessed with hindsight. Much of this dilemma lies within the dichotomy that I have mentioned before, between SA and LA practice. In Alfred Wights's day ('James Herriot') almost all practices were 'general' and 'mixed' and the individual vets could turn their hands to anything, but they are now very rare.

There was a professional rule at the time (which I believe has since been rescinded) that if any vet refused to turn out in emergency to a species with which he or she was totally unfamiliar, they nevertheless risked disciplinary action. So technically, a purely SA vet had no choice but to attend a calving or a colt with colic if requested, whether they had any experience of LA work or not. In both LA and SA spheres, practices have now become incredibly specialised, with species differentiation and consultancy-level exams in orthopaedics, dentistry, internal medicine, neurology, cardiology, ophthalmology, dermatology and many other detailed disciplines. Almost all practices are now brimming with vets holding certificates, diplomas and fellowships in these arcane areas and are highly qualified in their chosen specialties. This improves standards all over the veterinary world and is to the benefit of the practices as well as the patients and their owners.

Although the concept of specialization was in its early stages, I was very interested in dermatology and although I had no post-graduate diploma in it, I developed a small reputation among local colleagues who sent me referred cases. I must say immediately that, since many skin diseases are incurable or can only be kept under control, the colleagues often just needed a second opinion to reassure owners that the diagnosis was correct and the most that was possible was being done.

A good example was the perennial problem of fleas. These are strange little critters and often misunderstood by the animal-owning public. We are regularly asked, 'Why can one dog or cat be covered in fleas and not bothered, while another may have just a few and scratch itself raw?' Or, 'I've used a flea powder and a spray on him; why can't I get rid of them?' The answer lies in understanding individual reactions to fleas, and their life cycle.

Fleas don't actually spend much time on the animals themselves. They hop on for a blood meal, run around a bit and then hop off again, but prefer to live within the warmth and comfort of the animals' bedding and immediate environment. And if not their bedding, it will be upholstered chairs, sofas, carpets or even the owners' own beds, if they're allowed on them. It is there that the fleas mate and lay their eggs, which hatch and go through a few larval stages before becoming biting, feeding adults.

You may not spot fleas on some animals with thick coats, but you will see the evidence of them having been there. Having fed on blood, the fleas poo into the coat, and what they excrete looks like tiny black bits of coal dust. You can distinguish them from anything else by brushing some onto a wettened piece of kitchen paper and when they absorb the water, they stain the paper red.

So flea control depends not just on treating the adult fleas on the dog or cat but in their environment too, where the eggs and the larval stages must also be eliminated. If there is a severe problem, this may involve throwing out and replacing the animal's bedding and any bits of carpet, rug or fabric that they like lying on. If that is difficult the alternative is a very hot wash, and then in both cases using a can of special environmental flea spray on anything that cannot be washed or replaced, such as expensive bedding and fitted carpets. Those treatments smell quite nasty, and I used to advise owners to use them very thoroughly just before going away for the day or a weekend, to avoid breathing in too much of the chemical.

The other point; the reason that some cats and dogs react dramatically to fleas though others don't, is that the former have become allergic to antigens in the fleas' saliva, as they bite to feed. We see animals that have become so distressed as a result of flea bite allergy that they scratch themselves almost down to the dermis. How one becomes allergic and not another is a mystery of immunology and is just as variable as reacting to house dust mites or certain pollens. Has this answered a long-standing query from any readers?

Old-fashioned 'mixed' practices did still exist and an example was one I worked at in 1997. It was owned by two older vets who had been rather thrown together after the dissolution of a different partnership and they decided to 'put up their plate' jointly. They were great gentlemen 'of the old school', rather like the one I had first met in Plymouth. Smartly tailored suits and the inevitable bow ties, with impeccable manners and they previously had been doing LA work.

Between them they had bought a terraced house in the centre of town and converted it (sort of) into a practice, with the consulting area being the old front room and its tiled fireplace still there. They would have readily admitted their lack of experience in SA work and it is quite true that they weren't expert at it in a technical sense, but the clients adored them for their humour, education and old-fashioned courtesy. One day I noticed one of them pouring developer fluid from the 'dark room' (which doubled as a 'light room' when the blinds were opened) into a large brown storage bottle.

I am going to go off on a tangent for a few pages here, if you will permit me, into a discussion about radiography, the machines involved and the production and processing of plates as they are germane to the main story. These days many vets have scanning facilities and computed results which no longer involve any 'wet' processing. But in those days all radiography was mechanical and a darkroom was necessary. I always thought radiography was fascinating so it's a bit of a hobby of mine, but if it's an area that doesn't row your boat, please skip to page 129.

. . .

X-rays are very high-frequency, low-wavelength electromagnetic emissions invisible to the eye and are capable of penetrating living tissue and often going straight through. They are produced by high voltages aimed at an internal tungsten plate, typically between 50,000 and 110,000 volts, producing directional X-rays and are therefore both essential for diagnosis and quite dangerous. They are selectively absorbed by body tissues as they pass through, with bone absorbing the most and soft tissues (such as thin limbs or organs containing a lot of air, such as the lungs) absorbing the least.

Radiography film (that we used to call 'plates' but were really better called 'gels', a little like modern-day acetates but green before exposure and mostly black afterwards) was impregnated, in dark conditions in the factory, with a minutely thin coating of silver bromide. Silver bromide is colourless but it is very unstable and exposure to light, to X-rays or practically any other electromagnetic source, makes it split into silver (which, in this form, is grey to black) and free bromine, which disperses away.

Exactly the same principle is used in black and white photography, the only difference being that a negative is produced which then has to be printed again onto silver bromide paper which creates the positive photo. The more 'radio-dense' tissue is (such as bones), the fewer X-rays get through and therefore the lighter the result on the image plate. Equally, very 'radiolucent' tissue such as thin parts of the body and certain organs, muscles or any other less dense areas, appear darker.

The glory of them is that you don't need a second printing as you would in photography because the 'negative' is the perfect one to examine. Bones show up white as they are in real life and all the other parts of the radiograph are either in various shades of grey or completely black, such as outside the animal where the rays have only passed through air.

X-ray machines are expensive to buy but quite how much one invests depends not only on the kind of radiography one will be doing but the extent to which one's investment will be repaid. My first machine was an ex-army portable model and had been used to radiograph soldiers in make-shift hospitals in the field. I only paid £200 (in 1973) for it but it proved an excellent machine, usually static in the clinic but also able to be put into the car for imaging horses in their stables, or out in the fields so long as we could get a cable there.

In that situation, its main use was for looking at the small but fragile bones within the horses' hooves that cannot be examined. Considering how hunters, show jumpers, eventers and steeplechasers come crashing down after high fences onto the sensitive bones encased within their small hooves, it's a miracle that they don't break or damage them more often. There are three bones involved; the 'short pastern', the pedal or 'coffin' bone and the small navicular bone behind. And remember that in horses the hoof is effectively one single 'toe'; they have evolved for speed and moving on that central 'toe' creates the conditions for it.

But also the conditions for pathology. After the jump, the downward pressure is partly absorbed by the fetlock joint above, which flexes almost so much that it touches the ground and quite a lot of the rest of the shock must be absorbed by the foot. As a result, one encounters occasional fractures to these bones as well as a degenerative condition in the navicular bone which can result in chronic lameness. Only a radiograph can firmly diagnose these conditions and as soon as I saw that the practice was going to be a success I invested in a much more powerful machine, but there you are talking a lot more money if they are new. Most practices nowadays have sophisticated machines if not actually scanners.

Radiography plates came in two forms; either in light-tight envelopes which you could use immediately, or in packs where you had to open them in darkroom conditions to load them into cassettes. These are thin aluminium folders (of varying dimensions but frequently A3 to A5 size) with light-proof clips. There are certain types of visible light that do not affect radiographs; these are known as 'safe-lights' and are usually pale yellow or orange so that you can just about see what you are doing in the darkroom. Having adjusted the kilovoltage (kV), the higher it is, the more powerful the X-rays and the further they penetrate tissue. The milliamp-seconds (MaS) are then set which control the length of the exposure.

The development process, in the darkroom, is pretty simple. You either have three separate tanks or one split into three sections, plus a wash tank. You clip your film onto rectangular frames with little clothes peg-type clips to keep your hands away from the solutions (they are not dangerous, but unpleasant) and put it into the first tank, which is the 'developer'. When you take the film out of its cassette or open the envelope you can see no change to it compared with when it went in. What the developer does is 'catalyses' or enhances the dissociation of silver bromide into silver - 'develops' it, if you like. Having taken it out of the first tank you can see, in the glimmer of the safe-light, the image you wanted.

But now the process must be stopped, as there is still a lot of unchanged silver bromide which would immediately revert to silver if exposed to daylight. So having washed off the excess developer in the second tank (water), it goes into the third, known as 'fixer'. This is a solution of sodium thiosulphate in which silver bromide is very soluble so all the rest is dissolved away.

After a lot of use, fixer is quite rich in dissolved silver and it can be recovered by specialist companies. Then one only needs to wash it again in the final tank and you can switch the main lights on and hang them out to dry on things like small washing lines. In urgent cases they can be 'read' (examined) immediately when still wet, but more easily when they are dried and can be displayed on the radiograph reader.

However, there is a downer – a dangerous side to radiology. Because they are so utterly invisible to our eyes there is a habit of thinking they can't do much harm. X-rays occur in nature all the time. Our own sun produces them but they are mostly mopped up by our atmosphere before they hit us. And much denser bodies such as quasars produce fatal amounts of almost nothing else, but fortunately the majority are so many millions of light-years from us that their effect is not felt.

Yet, some years later I was doing a long locum in Martinique in the French-speaking part of the Caribbean. One day I had nothing to do for an hour and idly started looking through some of the old radiographs in a filing cabinet, and to my absolute HORROR saw that many of them had human hands (sometimes just fingers, but in others whole hands or even half an arm) on the plates.

I have already explained why almost all animals should be anaesthetised for radiography to avoid this, and the operators will step behind a lead-lined screen or special glass while the exposure is taken (X-rays cannot pass through lead). But in that practice, the nurses were being told to hold the animals still, under the direct beam. This is only ever justified if an anaesthetic is not possible, such as in very old or sick cases, though those often lie quietly anyway. If they really have to hold them, the operators must wear lead gloves and lead aprons to protect themselves. I saw a lead apron hanging from a door and found some gloves in a cupboard but the nurses said that the boss didn't insist on them being worn.

As one additional precaution, at least back in the UK, personnel had by law to wear 'exposure badges' which contain a small piece of radiograph film and were sent off for analysis every so often. Any member of staff showing positive must not go near the radiography suite for a fixed time.

When the Martinique boss (a white Parisian vet) was not around I questioned the nurses about it. They were lovely young folk – two guys and a girl – and all local but not only had they learned their work 'on the job' without exams or theory, but Henri had apparently never mentioned to them anything about the dangers of radiography or how to protect themselves.

At home the RVN training is detailed and extensive. The nurses have their own governing body, they are very well qualified and part of their training is radiography theory, practice and safety. These poor nurses had had no protection and no idea, when I asked them, how many radiographs they thought had been taken with their hands in them. I told them that while I was there, they were never to be in the direct beam and I would have a word with Henri about it. One remonstrated,

'Mais, carrément, la radio passe seulement à travers nos mains!' (Their first language was Créole but all the educated young people spoke French).

'But surely it can't be dangerous if the X-rays go straight through our hands!'

It was the moment to explain to them one last thing about ionising radiation. When I wrote that they either pass through the animal tissue or get absorbed, that only holds good for most of them. Some of them instead 'bounce' off the atomic nuclei in the tissue to the point that if you could see X-rays, on a single exposure, while most would go in the correct direction, some will splash outwards or back upwards like a jet of water hitting a sieve.

And those scattered rays, to anyone receiving enough of them over the space of years without protection, could not only cause cancer but, for the young female nurse, to damage the eggs in her ovaries. When the two male nurses asked whether it could affect their sperm, I said yes it could (though that was an exaggeration). They immediately crossed their legs, looked very uncomfortable and swore they'd never hold an animal down for radiography again. So even if theory may not have persuaded them, sex did.

To now return to the practice in England, I asked the partner why he was pouring the developer into the stock bottle from which it had come and he replied,

'Well, the darkroom is part of the X-ray room, and it's mostly bathed in daylight.' That was true, it was a small house and there certainly would not have been the opportunity of creating a separate darkroom.

'But we use the developer so little that it oxidises – it goes brown in the light and it becomes useless – we've spent pounds!' I told him that the answer would be to have a removable top made for the liquids to keep light out.

In that same practice, something else cropped up. I have already discussed neutering operations but not the mechanics of doing them and the operations of castration and spaying are one of the staples of a routine surgical day. Castration, either of male dogs, cats, rabbits and sometimes other species is a fairly simple operation (like everything else, what you do a lot and becomes routine, is 'simple'). However, in the case of big, over-boisterous dogs (part of the reason they were being castrated anyway) you have to be careful. In those large breeds, the testicles can be pretty hefty (I nearly wrote 'hairy') and you have to be quite sure that you have securely closed the major blood vessels, as it is difficult to stop them raising their blood pressure when tearing around in the days that follow. Animals can't be told to lie quietly in their beds for a week after major surgery.

Ovariohysterectomy, in female dogs and cats ('bitch spay' and 'cat spay') is a more difficult operation, especially in bitches. For one, the organs are inside the abdomen (unlike in uncomplicated castration) and for another, it is strangely tricky. I remember my first bitch spay un-supervised after Langford and it took me almost an hour, though, again, the more you do the faster you get. Much later my record for such an operation went down to nine minutes from first incision to last stitch, but that was on a good day; first job on the list and with a young and very slim case with no fat to plough through.

Mixing recent graduates with 'old hands', I should say that the average vet would need nearly half an hour, though there are some vets who dislike the operation so much that they won't do it at all. In any kind of surgical intervention, the quicker you can do it, the less time they remain under anaesthetic. And the less tissue damage and bleeding you cause, the quicker the recovery and the post-operative pain is minimised. When I told a human abdominal surgeon, he replied,

GOOD PRACTICES, NOT-SO-GOOD PRACTICES

'Nine minutes? That's exactly my record for a gall bladder remove.'

When I was getting back to that practice one day from some horse calls, the head nurse rushed out to me at the car, white as a sheet.

'John, I've got really bad news for you.'

'Oh no, I haven't been sacked again, have I?'

'No, I've had to book in a bitch spay.'

'Well, that's all right.'

'I've cancelled all the other operations.'

'Why?'

'How long will it take you, though?'

'About twenty minutes.'

'No, no; it's not a cat spay' (They are much quicker, by the way) 'It's a bitch spay.'

'Yes, I know. You can tell all the other op owners that they are «uncancelled».'

'Did you say twenty minutes?'

'Yes. Why do you think it would be longer?'

'Well, we've only ever done one here and both the vets did it together and it took them nearly two hours.'

'WHAT?'

'And they got through nearly a whole bottle of fluothane anaesthetic.' A few days later it was done, as well as three cat spays, a pin femur, two dentals and some bits and bobs. But it was all in all a good practice and I very much enjoyed working there. And their cheque was honoured.

I mentioned in an earlier chapter how it is human nature to assume that everyone else is familiar with their own town, computer system or the way the practice works, and in locums you see that all the time. Arriving in a strange town to work for a week or more is always a bit overwhelming especially if you arrive in the dark and have to start the next morning.

I did a three-week stint at a good practice in Kent, arriving on a wintery Friday evening on the train from London and the boss met me at the station. We drove in his car through rain to the main clinic while he explained to me that there were also two branch surgeries, one of which had a flat over it and that is where I would be staying. We picked up my practice car and he asked me to follow him the three miles to the branch and my new temporary home.

'OK, you start here tomorrow – Saturday - with a nine to eleven morning clinic, and then you come over to the main practice to start the weekend duty.'

'How do I get there?'

'You've just seen the road.'

'Well… yes… but going in the opposite direction, in the rain and dark, in a strange car and I was concentrating on following you.'

'But you'll recognise it.'

'With difficulty; there must have been at least six traffic lights.'

'I'll give you a map and you can follow that.' He went to get it from his car.

'Could we have a look at it? Where are we now? Circle the two surgeries and I'll do my best tomorrow to follow it and drive.'

He did so willingly enough but I could see that he already thought I was mentally defective for not naturally knowing my way around a major east Kentish town. At least it was light the following morning after the Saturday clinic at the branch and in those days before satellite navigation, with the help of the map I did find the main practice easily enough. There were three vets working there but they had all gone off for the weekend and the boss told me that for the two weekends I would be on my own, but as he lived on the premises he would be around to back me up if necessary. And, to be fair, I was given a weekday off in lieu to have a look around the area, so those were quite good conditions. In fact, out of the dozens of locum jobs I did, it was the only one where I was offered a weekday off.

The same happened in most locum practices when it came to getting to know the area or used to the computer system. In one I asked the secretary,

'The practice car is out of fuel; do you have an account at a petrol station?'

'Yes, at the BP garage.'

'Where's that?'

'After Tesco.'

'Sorry, where's Tesco?'

'You don't know where Tesco is?'

'Only arrived yesterday, haven't done any shopping yet.'

'OK, turn left out of here, go down the bypass, follow the signs to the town centre, go left at the first lights and it's in front of you at the roundabout.'

Here in France among the family, we call this 'Yvetot syndrome'. We were once at the small town in Normandy of that name and looking for the road to Rouen. We asked a local, who told us to go to 'la Poste' and turn right. 'Où se trouve la Poste?', we asked and he looked at us so pityingly as if we were the only people around so lobotomised as not to even know where the main post office in Yvetot was.

As for computers, in those locum days I encountered a large range of different (often quite recently installed) systems as the old routine of written records was being replaced. I imagine that when vets became digitalized, a good number of IT companies jumped onto the bandwagon and advertised their own systems to sell to practices and I don't think I ever came across exactly the same system twice.

I was computer-literate though, as in the mid-nineties I was writing up my MPhil dissertation on the system available at the time before Windows, called 'Word Perfect' on MS-DOS. This involved navigating without a touch screen, trackpad or mouse, using the twelve F keys at the top of the keyboard and it took a lot of learning compared with what we have now, such as the easy Word Office system which I am using for this. When I mentioned those F keys to Emma my IT-savvy nineteen-year-old in her second year of medicine, she replied, 'Oh, I wondered what they were for.'

It took a long time to master the MS-DOS system but, once again, like anything else that you do and use every day, it becomes 'easy' in a relative sense. Then you saved your work onto what they called a 'floppy' disc which actually was not floppy at all but like a thin CD encased in a rigid plastic jacket. To save, you were asked at the bottom of your screen (black and white and on one of those huge old-fashioned cathode-ray TVs) whether you wanted to save onto the 'C' drive or the 'A' drive.

When you were on someone else's computer - in this case it was the university's as I started by using early machines in the library - you had to make sure you entered 'A' drive so that it saved onto your floppy. Once at the end of a long writing-up session, I was tired and entered 'C' by mistake to find that I'd saved a day's work onto the uni's central server and spent part of the next day at their IT centre trying in vain to track it down, but as I hadn't identified it correctly it was lost.

Then to write the rest I bought my first PC, second-hand ex-office; an Intel 286 with the <u>stupendous</u> processor power of 9MHz, which I upgraded to a 486 as they became available with 128 <u>huge</u> KB! People really did brag in those days that they'd just bought the latest version with … yes … a whopping thirty megabytes! A heavy bit of kit that took up, with the keyboard and screen, all your desk with a millionth of the computing power of an iPhone now.

My experiences in locum practice in being shown how to use their new IT system varied a lot. In some, the secretary or boss patiently gave me at least half an hour to explain its complexities (and often, idiosyncracies) whereas in others it was a rushed nurse with all sorts of activity going on around us, trying to do the whole thing in ten minutes. If I were to conflate many conversations with many members of staff in lots of practices, the synthesis might be the following:

'Ruth, could you come and look at my screen? I did the same as last time but it's gone blank.' Daggers looks from the secretary as if I'd just called up the dark web or the Penthouse page.

'I showed you how to do that yesterday.'

'Yes, I'm really sorry.'

'OK, click on the right and get the toolbar.'

'I see, I clicked on the toolbar at the top.'

'No, that toolbar's for something else, you don't need it.'

'Up to speed on that.'

'So, double-click yeah? And you get the… oh, it's not supposed to do that…'

'Ah…'

'Why have I got a blank page?'

'Er…'

'Right, when that happens click on Escape, then you're back on the first page, then PR for practice records.'

'I wanted consultation charges.'

'Don't rush me, all in good time, yes enter CC for that.'

'OK.'

'Now I can't get CC… Sue? Are you on the consultation charges page?… can you come off it for a moment?… because sometimes if it's up on one screen it doesn't show on the other.'

'Yes, I see…'

But you don't see, well not completely. By that time, you are either behind the person who has come to your aid and is sitting in front of the screen, or you are standing slightly to one side. In either case, you don't get such a good view as they do and you are simultaneously looking at the screen, what they are doing with their mouse, how many clicks and whether they were left or right.

And people so used to a system and having navigated it so many times aren't always the best at slowing down so that you can follow them. I always felt very embarrassed at having to interrupt busy people in the first three or four days of arriving at each practice and I always did get quite slick at them in the end, even though it was often soon before I left at the end of my week or fortnight. In one I did ask this question, though,

'How long has the IT been in place?'

'It went in last year.'

'It's a good system, though; how long did it take you all to get used to it?'

'Oh, months.' I rest my case.

One of the nurses in Kent that Saturday afternoon asked me to look at a young GSD (German Shepherd dog) that had been admitted that morning with a painful abdomen. They had radiographed her and the results were inconclusive so they had left her for the locum (me) to sort out over the weekend. The other vets were all younger, and I am sure in a technical sense superior to me, but we had been very well trained in palpating (feeling in detail) an abdomen and a good clinical examination. The moment I touched her tummy it was clear that something bad was happening in there although it was quite right that the blood results and radiographs did not help.

I had seen many cases in my career of 'obstructive intestinal foreign bodies' (things stuck in the guts, basically). Dogs are notorious for swallowing all manner of objects. I have removed two large solid rubber balls from a single stomach in another GSD, plus any number of toys, stones, sponges, bits of metal or plastic, socks, knucklebones and one doll's head.

Some of these showed up well on radiographs and others not but in all cases, they had become jammed in the stomach or intestine. The huge ones (how does a dog swallow a heavy, solid rubber object the size of a cricket ball?) remain in the stomach and may not show symptoms unless they obstructed the outflow to the duodenum. The rest pass the duodenal sphincter and then generally either become wedged in the small intestine or further down, at the narrow ileo-caecal valve before becoming the wider large intestine.

Some foreign bodies, particularly the smoother ones, can and do travel slowly down the intestine and if they don't halt completely, they will be eventually voided. Others cause a lot of trauma as they move down and it's dispiriting, having seen where the foreign body is, to see lengths of purplish, damaged gut above the blockage. There you have to decide whether to rely on natural healing (the gut has a huge blood supply and can heal very well) or resect that part of the intestine (cutting the damaged area out completely and re-joining the ends) but that is a finely-balanced decision. If you leave it to resolve naturally and it doesn't do so, you risk a perforated gut and probably death. If you resect too willingly, you have interfered unnecessarily and increased the chance of infection through spillage.

In all cases, the animal stops eating, vomits profusely and becomes dehydrated. In this particular one I suspected something soft, but, curiously, it seemed to be involving almost all the gut. I did an exploratory laparotomy (fancy words for opening up the abdomen) and found it was much worse than I had thought.

The entire gut, from stomach to large intestine was tightly concertinaed-up and in spasm. The first enterotomy incision (opening the intestine itself) revealed multiple thick strands of an apparently synthetic material that were blocking the intestine and prevented peristalsis (the normal movement of the intestine from top to bottom moving digested food along). And in one part, intussusception had occurred where one section of the intestine had telescoped into another. I did a gastrotomy (opening the stomach) and about six enterotomies (opening the intestine), cutting the threads at each point until I had removed all of the material and repaired them and the intussusception before I could close.

Faecal material (the contents of the intestine) is always released in these operations however careful you are and how many bowel clamps you apply. With so many separate enterotomies we didn't have enough clamps on that day so post-operative infection is a real risk and we used heavy antibiotics and gamma-globulins.

Changing clothes afterwards (your scrubs only protect

your shirt and trousers to an extent in really messy ops) and ringing the owners, the source of the material was revealed. They told me that she had to be left during the daytime when they were at work and she had started to chew an old sofa in her den – well, she had more or less wrecked it. Dogs often do this when missing their owners especially when they are young. They thought she may have swallowed some of it but had no idea it was that much. She recovered uneventfully, the sofa went to the dump and they arranged for someone to call from time to time to keep her company during the day, so apart from the owners being a thousand pounds or so worse off it was a good resolution.

After that marathon op, I was told that the Saturday early evening surgery for urgent cases had started and there were three clients already waiting for me. I shot into the consulting room but the kind nurse popped a cup of coffee in front of me having realised that I was in a strange practice, had had no lunch and hadn't stopped since that morning. Little gestures like that made all the difference especially when, having arrived, you go straight into work and have had no time to take a breath, look around and see where you are. And when we'd finished and cleaned up, she did escort me with her car to the dual carriageway towards my digs as by that hour it was dark outside and raining again.

When I sold my practice, I applied to and was accepted at the University of Southampton to read French and Spanish. I already had an A level in French and four years later got my BA in those two languages having spent the third (abroad) year in Granada, Spain. But towards the end of the first year in Southampton, a peculiar series of coincidences took place.

I have written of some of my exploits in the French Antilles and it came about because in the French department I had become friendly with Nathalie, a postgrad from Martinique on secondment to the department for a year. She was half white French and half 'Antillaise' with that beautiful golden skin and she was very excited about her forthcoming marriage to Philippe, the scion of a wealthy Parisian banking family.

They were to be married at her old parish church in Martinique and then after their honeymoon in Tahiti they would live in one of the family houses in the posh Third Arrondissement. We'd talked so much together about it although she had never exactly invited me, but just before she left she said 'You're coming, John, of course, aren't you?' Paying my way through university and with no grant I wasn't quite in the league of jetting off to a two-day wedding in the Caribbean without any other reason to go, so I decided to try for a locum job over there at the same time.

Information in those pre-google days being harder to get than it is now, I wrote in French to the Embassy in London for a list of the vet practices in Martinique. I didn't expect a quick answer (or even one at all) but an embossed envelope from them arrived by return, with a list of the practices and completed, before the signature, with 'Confraternellement'. This is a tricky word to translate but in essence, means 'with best wishes from a colleague' and certainly is not a way of finishing a letter to a stranger. And on top of the letter was his name as 'chargé d'affaires'; a French vet, of all people working in the Embassy. I wrote to all the practices on the list but heard nothing for a month.

In the meanwhile Professor Ettinghausen, head of Spanish, had asked me if I was interested in a summer job at the University of Salamanca in June after the exams and through the whole of July. However, this would clash with the locum job if I got a reply. Still nothing in the post, but then came the second coincidence. I had to decide one way or another by a certain date; that day arrived and with still nothing from the Caribbean, I signed yes. To then get home that evening to find a letter with French stamps confirming a job for July and August near Fort-de-France, the capital. I rang Henri, the boss, and told him that alas I could now only do August and most of September (term re-started at the beginning of October) and at first he said forget it, but then changed his mind and I was hired.

Salamanca is the most beautiful city in western Spain and I loved the job, but it was a rush at the end, as by the first of August I was taking the bus to Madrid, flight to Heathrow, train to home, one day back to wash and repack my clothes before Channel ferry, train and finally flight from Paris. Nathalie was delighted and offered to put me up over the wedding weekend with neighbours as it was quite a distance from the practice where I was lodged and I took a three-day weekend off.

The marriage was fabulous if sweltering inside the church, though most of the day was spent outside. While there I got to know Nathalie's best friend from the Sorbonne, a girl called Nanou. She must have told me she was from Normandy but I don't remember asking her which part. I drove her to the airport on Monday after the wedding for her return to Paris and that appeared to be that, until the third coincidence. A year later I was staying in Le Havre with a friend, Fabrice, and he mentioned that he wanted to drive over to see his best mate François. And there outside, just getting into her car, was Nanou. Exclamations of amazement from both of us and if she'd left two minutes earlier, I would never have seen her again or known that she was François' sister. These things seem so weird that they move into the realm of metaphysics, don't they?

After the French and Spanish degree, I was offered partial funding to study for an MPhil in linguistics and, enjoying myself rather too much, managed to make that last four years. In the meanwhile, during some of the vacations, I continued doing locums. The two last ones before I resigned my MRCVS and left the profession were in 2003, and they were the best of all.

The first was in Penygraig, a sweet little town just below Tonypandy in south Wales. There I worked with the first and only UK male vet nurse in my career and very competent he was too. All the staff were good fun and full of an earthy 'valleys' humour.

'We'd better get back to the surgery or the boss will have our guts for pit props.' Running, I stumbled on something,

'Enjoy your trip?'

'Ouch, I've hurt my ankle.'

'Could have been worse.'

'How?'

'Could have been me.'

Or, calling a nurse into the consulting room,

'Mae, I need a hand.'

'Ask me tidy.'

'Sorry, could you come in please?'

'That's better love,' (always pronounced 'lev'). And then later when the client had gone,

'Thanks for that, Mae.'

'You're not a bad vet, boyo, even if you are English.'

I loved the way they finished their sentences with 'is

it?', as in, 'You all right John, is it?' or 'We'd better park over by there, is it?' and it took me back to Hiatt Baker in Bristol when Mike, a Welsh mate a few doors down came into my room one evening looking glum. He was doing a degree in maths.

'Are you all right, Mike?'

'Can't do me sums.'

'Is that what you call them?'

'It's what me mam calls them – doin' all right with yer sums, lev, is it?'

The whole area around that part of the world is fascinating, a combination of the remains of the old mining industry and stunning scenery. Just walking up to Tonypandy one lunchtime I was amazed how open and pleasant people were to a total stranger and how many wished me a good afternoon. A kind and decent race, the Welsh. There were many of them at Bristol (just over the border from the 'Principality' as they insisted on calling it) and I never met one whom I didn't like. The new Severn bridge was just being completed during our time there and over mugs of coffee, it was endlessly discussed.

'If you think about it, like, this means that England has become part of Wales.'

'Yes, but the toll booths are on the English side so the bridge is English.'

'Ah well, that's intentional you see, because it means that us Welsh can go all the way across, but then before we have to pay, we may be so heartbroken at leaving the Principality, we can do a U-turn and enjoy the view twice for nothing.'

At Bristol I went out with a girl from a nice little town called Ystrad Mynach, north of Caerphilly, and to visit one day, had been told to get to 'Hengoed' and then follow the signposts. One such pointed straight across at a farm gate and there were a lot of vehicle tracks. Accordingly, I opened the gate, drove in, shut it after me and crossed the field. Indeed, on the other side, there was the short-cut road to Ystrad to visit Lynn and the Thomas family. They don't come any sweeter.

It was at the Penygraig practice where I encountered one case that did completely elude me and I have to admit I was very embarrassed about it. Cryptorchidism means 'a hidden testicle'; and we see it from time to time in all species, and this particular one was in a dog. He had just one external testicle; the assumption being that the other one is in the abdomen somewhere. Cryptorchid dogs are often highly sexed and it is the main reason for requesting their castration. This is because the 'retained' testicle is in a much warmer place than lying where it should be, outside the abdomen in the cooler scrotal sac and as a consequence produces much more of the male hormone testosterone. Yet despite this, retained testicles can be remarkably tiny.

I operated, removed the external one first and then opened the abdomen to search for the undescended one. Absolutely in vain. I looked for the best part of an hour but simply could not find it. There were only two possibilities. Either I was losing my touch and it was time I threw my gloves into the bin for good, or that particular dog was one of those rare cases who only had one testicle from the beginning. I never did find out, as the downside to being a locum is that you can't follow up on your cases.

In any event, my life as a locum during university vacations was moving to an end. At Southampton I then met Anne, a French post-grad from the University of Rouen who was working as a 'lectrice' (French language assistant) and studying there for her Master's. We married in 2000 having come to live in France and by 2003 she was pregnant with our first daughter, Emma. We had already decided that she would go straight back to work as a teacher at a '*Lycée*' in Le Havre when her maternity leave expired, and as we were determined to have one full-time parent at home, that was going to be me. Her sister Manon arrived three years later, and those years as being house-husband and at-home dad were the most fulfilling of my life. I loved every second of them and it was a rare privilege, as a man, to have the chance to spend all my day with our two children.

But there was just time to fit in one last locum a month before Emma was born and with that one, I went full circle; back to near my childhood, in Penzance. We had been there on holiday from Plymouth and it was enchanting to return. Another town in the spirit of Tonypandy, where the people were smiling and welcoming. Strolling on the promenade by the sea on the Sunday afternoon when I arrived, once again folks would spontaneously say 'Good afternoon' or 'Lovely, isn't it?'. The practice was smart and well-managed by a husband-and-wife vet team taking a fortnight's holiday, I shared a pretty little cottage on the seafront with a locum from New Zealand, the work was not particularly demanding and the owners were nice. A perfect way to end.

So that is an overview of some practices. As in the whole of human life and behaviour, there are 'good'uns', and bad'uns' and often just 'all right'uns'. But in the whole thirteen years I spent doing part- time locums I am glad to report that, with the few exceptions, the practices were well-run and clean with skilled, motivated staff who were a pleasure to work with.

CHAPTER 6
THERAPIES

One of the overwhelming aspects of medical therapy is the plethora of meds listed in the veterinary pharmacopaeas. A year of pharmacology at Bristol and all the updates, yet there seemed to be so many meds that you simply didn't recognise. One reason for this is that many of the molecules that make the newer drugs we use are simply very slight improvements on the existing range, depending on how aggressively they are marketed. And each med often has a huge number of different trade names. One of the major aspects of this (brought out in Ben Goldacre's fascinating - and worrying - book 'Bad Science', which anyone interested in big pharma, herbal products, pretend scientists and alternative therapies ought to read) is the extent to which the need for therapy is exaggerated for commercial gain.

There is, for example, a group of antibiotics called fluoroquinones (or 'quinolones'), marketed under about fifteen brand names as being the antibiotic of choice in certain 'gram negative' infections such as bronchitis and urinary infections. But the big downer - and one the reps keep very quiet about - is that in some cases they can cause as a side effect the tearing or complete rupture of the Achilles tendon. Yet these antibiotics are still being prescribed as a result of heavy commercial marketing, although simpler and cheaper alternatives are available.

I got on well with all the 'drug reps' who called at the surgery; they often brought news of new approaches to therapy that you may not have had time to read in the veterinary press, gave out free samples and in general if I had the time, they were a pleasure to have a cup of tea with. They also proved an interesting source of gossip and general news from other practices and the profession in general, something which if you are working on your own is welcome.

One such, Romney Jackson, has remained a close friend to this day and who after his rep days developed his skills to become a consultant immunologist. Some of the reps were vets, some RVNs; most had degrees and were well informed. I became particularly friendly with the staff from a nearby manufacturing company, Duphar, based in premises at West End, near Southampton, and the following tale may prove enlightening.

I had been approached by two vet colleagues, Peter Hall-Patch of Hythe and Richard Orton of Fordingbridge, who had in their turn been asked for their help by a lady called Ann Hyland, the leading light in the recently-formed British Endurance Horse and Pony Society (BEH-PS). This was a group that, within very strict veterinary supervision, organised treks of up to a hundred miles as an ultimate test of the fitness of both horse and rider. There was another association, called the 'Golden Horseshoe' in the USA but they, unfortunately, had had several horses die after their events, so we were determined not to let that happen in BEHPS.

Ann wanted a new veterinary approach devised to detect hidden exhaustion when we examined all the horses and ponies at different points of the course, to eliminate overtired or stressed ones. Horses are such faithful creatures and often so determined to do their best for their riders that they push themselves beyond the point of exhaustion. So I, Peter, and Richard got together on a couple of evenings to start from scratch and decide how often the examinations should take place, and what we should be looking at to ensure that no horse went beyond the limit of its natural endurance.

On one of the 100-mile marathons across the New Forest, I was accompanied by one of the drug reps, a delightful chap called Richard Jacobs from Duphar, who had not long before detailed me a new form of electrolyte ('drip') for dehydration in large animals. He was very enthusiastic about it (well they have to be) and I had ordered quite a large stock.

The procedure was that we eliminated any horse and rider combination that we, by the parameters that we had created, felt should go no further. Those were sent to rest at an equine centre that Anne Hyland had hired, taken there by horsebox. Their owners were obliged to stay awake with any eliminated horse the whole night and to call one of us vets, still on-site, if they were worried. Many cases of over-exertion shock could be delayed; a horse could look fine at the end or if stopped on a technicality but become ill in the night. In the event, all the riders chose to stay awake or at least get up several times in the night to look at their mounts, whether they had been eliminated or not.

Problems happened just three times in the events I attended. In one, Richard and I were asleep in our bunks in a caravan and an owner rushed in and said 'Come quickly, she's collapsed and she's breathing badly.' This had been one of the mares that had completed the course unremarkably and we had been happy with that evening. In cases like these, there is often unnoticed dehydration and fluid therapy is usually effective. There are all sorts of commercial brands of electrolytes marketed by multiple companies, but I decided to use the one sold by Duphar as the best choice. Richard almost went to pieces.

'But she looks so ill!... do you think you can save her? Oh God, she's so pale.' Once I got the drip going, I said:

'But Richard, a few months ago you were confidently telling me that your electrolyte was the answer to exactly this form of dehydration.'

'Yes, I know but that's what they detail us to say. I've never actually seen it in use.'

His product worked beautifully and after the third litre, given more gradually, the mare got up, seemed none the worse for her shock and got on with a bran mash. Incidentally, the three of us got together one last time, wrote an article about it, submitted it to the *Veterinary Record* to be considered for publication and it was accepted. Later we had a letter from the British Veterinary Association (BVA) saying that we had won something called the William Hunting Award for the best article published that year written by general practitioners. I had never heard of it, though I knew that William Hunting had been one of the pioneer vets of the profession. Richard told me on the phone that it was the highest honour they could bestow on a GP and I later drove up to BVA Congress in Lancaster to receive it on behalf of the three of us, as the others were not available. And got back in time for evening surgery in Romsey, too, having spent about twenty minutes at the conference.

In the mid-1970s a new 'anaesthetic' agent called Immobilon was manufactured and released. I put it in inverted commas as, to be technically correct, it was not a true anaesthetic but a profound narcotic and was said to be forty times as potent as heroin. Its generic name was etorphine and it acted as an inducing agent (to make the animal go down) and was also profoundly analgesic (painkilling) so although the horse or donkey would continue making some reflex movements during surgery, they were not generally associated with the painful parts of an operation.

Prior to its release to the veterinary market, equine anaesthesia was a tricky and sometimes risky business in general practice and mostly done outside. This contrasted sharply with vet school's equine surgery units, as a visit to the LA theatres at any of the schools will prove. There they have huge opening doors to admit species as tall as giraffes and lifts and hoists to place the anaesthetised animals onto vast hydraulic tables. Animals are routinely induced intravenously, then intubated (a huge endotracheal tube that goes into the windpipe) and kept under for the duration of the surgical intervention. All these under the eye of experts; a team of at least one consultant in equine surgery and a veterinary anaesthetist, as well as equine nurses, grooms and other staff.

I only ever saw one horse there that accidentally 'came to' in the middle of an operation at a university and it was both dangerous and startling. In fact, the truth is that it was indirectly my fault. I had referred a very complex femoral fracture in a Doberman dog to Langford, where there were four separate breaks and any number of smaller fractured pieces and the surgery was quite beyond my ability.

Out of interest I took the afternoon off and drove up to the hospital. Having watched the fractures being expertly reduced and plated by the resident SA orthopaedic surgeon, I had an hour to spare and watched an equine operation in the LA theatre. The thoroughbred had already been 'put under' and Dr. Alistair Barr was doing an endoscopy examination. I got chatting to the anaesthetist, Dr. Barbara Weaver who had taught us when we were students. She had been one of the pioneers of research in modern veterinary anaesthesia and was quite a character.

We had been nattering about my time at Langford; who had left, who was still around and general gossip and I am sure, with hindsight, that I distracted her. The horse, which had been upside down on the table, suddenly began to regain consciousness, started to thrash around and then fell off it, with Professor Pearson shouting at Alistair to get out of the way. The horse then coughed out his endotracheal tube and shakily stood up. Fortunately, Alistair had finished but it was an unpleasant moment. I had to leave to get home and never did admit to the staff there my partial guilt, so if any of them remember the incident, I apologise.

Anaesthesia is quite different in the field, of course. Apart from in the specialised private equine clinics where they operate at their permanent theatres with all the equipment, for the smaller practices an alternative has to be found. One primitive method, in frequent use until I qualified, was a specially-made leather mask into which a pad containing liquid chloroform was placed and the horse was walked until it went down. It was successful in experienced hands but chloroform is easy to over-dose and you have to be very vigilant.

Various other agents were also in use, one of which was called chloral hydrate, a cousin of chloroform which was given intravenously but where a slight overdose could result in respiratory depression and it also needed to be 'topped up'; tricky when you are scrubbed up and trying to keep your hands sterile.

However, when Immobilon came along it was the answer to our prayers (with one - very important - caveat which you will see below). It could be administered quite easily intravenously in the field and, uniquely then, there was an antidote to it (Revivon, or diprenorphine) which was given also intravenously at the end, and the horse came to and stood up almost immediately. They are sweaty and a bit shaken when they rise, but perfectly conscious and without the staggering around which was involved in recovery from many other anaesthetics. Causing immobilisation for about half an hour, it was perfect for gelding, stitching wounds and for any other procedure which was fairly quick.

In one case I had been called to a horse who was outside in a fenced paddock but he could not be persuaded to walk and was very depressed. I arrived; he looked in agony and there was dried blood between his hind legs. Feeling higher, I touched something large and wooden. The owner ran to the other side of the paddock and saw the remains of half a fence post where he had presumably tried to jump out. I gave him Immobilon and pulled out a piece of post thirteen inches long and four inches thick which had gone straight up into his groin, but by a miracle had not penetrated the artery or any nerves. Stitching was impossible but the wound, being in a folded position, retracted to something quite small. With local application followed by daily antibiotics and protection against fly eggs being deposited, he made an uneventful recovery.

Immobilon also got me out of a dilemma on a night call when I didn't have experienced help to take with me, such as one of the nurses. A pig farmer rang to say that one of his boars had got in with another and had gored his ham open right down to the bone. It was indeed a huge injury and he had bled extensively, though he was still standing. I needed a short-acting anaesthetic that would not depress his already low blood pressure because of the haemorrhage, but Immobilon had really not been tested much on pigs. I checked the datasheet and read that it could be used for them but the dosage was yet uncharted territory.

As you will see in the following paragraphs, the dose of Immobilon (on a ml. per kilo bodyweight basis which is how injectable meds are usually calculated) varies hugely between species, and particularly in one very important species, which I will come to. As students we had several lectures on how to assess the weight of all the domestic LA species; young and old, fat and thin, as weighing them was usually impossible. Small animals, of course, we could weigh on scales. I gave the boar slightly less than the computed dose per kilo for a horse and he lay down very quietly, breathed well (though etorphine, like all opiates, can cause respiratory depression) and permitted me with no apparent pain to put in the stitches to return the laid-open ham to one piece. He looked so peaceful when I finished that I decided not to use the antidote and left him to recover slowly. The farmer rang the next morning to say that he was up and eating.

We had been told that certain species were very much more, or very much less, sensitive to etorphine, than others. For instance, by trial and error it was established that a huge mammal such as a rhinoceros could be felled by the same dose as we would give to a small pony, but for practical reasons the effective doses were difficult to establish among the species.

A vet who qualified in the same year as me had been using the drug in a field and then there was a trek back involving climbing over a couple of stiles. All the syringes and drug vials as well as the equipment had been dropped into a cardboard box and he was carrying that box under his arm back to the car. Halfway back, the vet collapsed and started to go blue. Someone noticed that the needle of the Immobilon syringe was sticking out through the cardboard box that he had carried, but surely the tiny amount left within a syringe needle could not knock a man out? He was too young and fit to have had a heart attack so they took a risk and gave him a small dose of the antidote, and he recovered though reported feeling weird for several days.

Of course, it would have been impossible to test Immobilon on people during its development stage so nobody had any idea what effect it may have on a human subject. Even before that specific case we were very wary of it, but at the beginning we were all trying it out in practical situations for the first time and establishing our own routines. I found that I had about six seconds after giving it intravenously before it started to take effect.

The owner (or a nurse) held the head collar at the outset because you need both hands for the intravenous; one to raise the jugular vein by pressing below it just above the shoulder, and the other to get the needle into the vein and inject. That gave little time to put the safety cap back onto the needle as any fiddling could result in self-injection. In some cases, I quickly put the cap back on and passed it to my nurse whom I trusted to handle it properly. Or if I was alone, I threw the empty syringe without its cap away onto an empty patch of grass at a distance and told everybody not to touch it.

Following the i/v, I would then take charge of the horse or donkey on my own and told the others to get out of the way because the danger is that they can fall on you. When large creatures are anaesthetised, they may slowly crumple downwards in which case you are safe, or they may fall away from you which is also fine.

But if a horse weighing between 350 and 600 kilos falls on top of you it's serious. An experienced Irish equine vet I knew from Salisbury had been killed a year earlier when such a case fell on him. The horse trapped his nurse, too, but she was slightly further away and was pulled to safety. With Immobilon, having taken the head collar and told everyone to keep clear, I would pull the horse forward into a walk for a few steps, then it did so faster of its own volition as the drug kicked in. Then as it started to fall down forwards, I would sharply pull its head around towards me so that it always fell away from me.

But geldings (castration of male horses) did not always go as smoothly as that, and just about the most traumatic day of my practising life happened in Martinique. I should explain that at Langford we had had padded recovery boxes adjacent to the LA theatres and in practice there were times when we would have given anything for them. Large animal recovery from general anaesthesia can be gradual and calm where they slowly come to, lift their heads in a 'what happened to me?' sort of way, don't try to stand too quickly and eventually get up, shaky but otherwise normal. Or the opposite; very nervous animals' recovery may be violent and quite frightening to watch and they should be somewhere enclosed and soft. When an animal weighing more than half a ton starts to cart off unsteadily it is serious and they are so strong that human restraint is often useless.

On that particular afternoon in Martinique, I was asked to do a gelding on a big stallion at a new property that had been built on a large ledge, halfway up into the high central jungle. There was a beautiful view of the valleys below and the beaches in the distance, but also a sheer, cavernous drop. And the garden wasn't even fenced. I told the owner straight away that it was a terrible place to do the operation, especially on such an excitable creature. Apparently he was unpredictable at the best of times and became a raving nutcase anywhere near a mare on heat, which was the reason for the operation in the first place.

It was the first gelding I had done on the island and had asked Henri what horse anaesthetic agents he had. He replied that he usually used chloral hydrate but he was waiting for deliveries from France. Otherwise, all that was left was some ketamine. I was very worried about using it on that horse, and even more so about doing it so close to a precipice. But the owner was adamant that it had to be done up there and it was true that it would have been a long walk down over poor roads with an intractable creature, to find more extensive flat ground. We also need hot water and sometimes electricity so being near a house is an advantage.

It started well; he went down quickly to the highest intravenous dose I dared give and the operation itself was uneventful, but on recovery he became violently agitated and as he tried to get up, he staggered towards the ledge. It took four of us pulling on the rope and head collar to half turn him back towards us and one of the guys then attached the long rope to a brick pillar that seemed to support the front of the house. He was right on the edge with only three legs on it and I was thinking 'Oh God I hope that pillar is a solid concrete post inside or he'll be off the side and most of the house will fall down.' Thank heavens he regained his balance, saw where he was and then stood still. Everyone gets flashbacks and that one is my all-time worst.

. . .

Therapies

The speed of the antidote to Immobilon – diprenorphine - also made it possible to operate on a number of cases in one session. One afternoon soon after I had set up in Romsey, a horse owner of a Romany persuasion had asked me to geld seven very skinny thoroughbred colts in a single afternoon, one after the other. I admit I was pretty desperate for work; he had asked my nurse for a quote on the phone and we had told him it would be £90 for the lot (a trifling sum now, but this was in 1974, so I suppose the fee was the equivalent of over a thousand these days). It went to plan and at the end he said,

'What do I owe you then, sir?'

'Ninety pounds.'

'How much?'

'Wasn't that what was agreed on the phone?'

'Yeah, but ninety quid, that's a lot of money, sir.' I was beginning to feel quite embarrassed when he suddenly let out a great guffaw, fished in his back pocket and pulled out the biggest roll I'd ever seen. He thumbed off the tenners and then one more, saying 'Make it the ton, that's a good job, sir.' He probably sold the geldings for five hundred apiece and good luck to him.

All new therapies are the fruit of research which is of the highest importance, though some of it is in such arcane corners of science that it is tempting to ask how much of it is applicable to practical animal health and care. You will not see many research papers like 'New approaches to plating the humerus'; they are more likely to be a version of 'Actions of kainate and ACPH selective glutamate receptor ligands on group 11 mGlu antagonist LY379268.'

A lot of these infinitesimally specialised areas do impact on real medicine and surgery, but then again academic researchers, aided by their graduate students in all faculties all over the world rely on research output for their funding, reputations and promotion. I do not want to hazard a guess here at what proportion of it is really useful to clinical practice. For one thing, this would be impossible to assess but also that I would risk comments from the universities in the form of, 'Those GPs, what do they know, with their arms up cattle and emptying dogs' anal glands; we're the cutting edge here.' And they would have a point.

Antibiotics and steroids were in my time - and still are - the basis of a large percentage of medical therapy, and it is amazing how little it has substantially changed. Huge ranges of new antibiotics were created in the early days following the first ones in the 1930s with Fleming's accidental discovery of penicillin and the German laboratory Bayer's equally fortuitous discovery of sulphonamides when they were actually working on dyes and happened to notice that they had an anti-bacterial action. Both of these drug groups saved thousands of lives from infection and gangrene during and after the Second War. But since the 1970s, apart from playing with molecules to make slight improvements, the truth is that hardly any really different, revolutionary antibiotics have come onto the market.

Bacterial resistance has become a curse and the really nasty bacteria such as MRSA refer to resistance to Methicillin which was developed last century. Another major hospital-acquired infection, Clostridium difficile has become almost untreatable and these days if you go into a hospital for a minor procedure you may end up worse than when you went in, or dead.

The situation is similar in the case of glucocorticoids, better known as corticosteroids, or more simply, steroids. These were first synthesised in the 1950s and prednisolone, dexamethasone, betamethasone and occasionally the more potent fluorinated steroids such as clobetasol have not changed much since. They figure, with antibiotics, in the majority of routine prescriptions today, seventy years later.

The word 'steroids' as a group also contains the mineralocorticoids and the anabolic steroids. The latter are useful in veterinary therapy for old and debilitated animals. No, they don't start growing huge muscles, pumping iron and dying early. But they are useful in encouraging flagging kidneys and other organs to work a bit harder in very old animals and give the owners just a little bit longer with their pets until the end. I will return to this sad area in the final chapter.

Research may also involve experimental animals, particularly on new vaccines and new molecules, before they pass to the testing stage where they are first tried on humans. I have previously mentioned the testing protocol for the canine viral disease, parvovirus. Adult dogs were better at resisting it, but litters of puppies were easily infected and many died of dehydration, passing revolting blood-flecked diarrhoea with a very characteristic smell. Being viral, there was no treatment and at the time there was no vaccine, and the only way we could help was with intravenous therapy. But in puppies, electrolytes are in a practical sense very difficult to administer. In the interim, a veterinary virologist spotted that a cat disease, feline panleucopaenia, was also a parvovirus. There was a vaccine for that, which is routinely given to kittens together with the two forms of cat 'flu and viral leukaemia, and is regularly boosted in adult cats.

However, the ethical question was: should we give a cat vaccine to dogs? Reasoning that it was better than letting them die, we all tried a few doses in dogs that were at risk and there was no adverse reaction. It became the norm for a few months and we hoped that the cat vaccine would at least reduce the severity of the symptoms in dogs.

In fact, it proved quite protective and I didn't see one case of parvovirus in dogs inoculated with the cat vaccine. As I described above, the pure dog vaccine testing was wrecked and had to be re-started and the suppliers ran quickly out of the cat vaccine due to the demand. I was lucky in that I had just ordered a thousand doses and my stock held out until the first proper dog vaccine was marketed. It is now routinely included in all puppy inoculations and boosters and is the 'P' in the 'DHLP' routine vaccine.

I was rather thrown once when Kirsty, a six-month-old flat-coat retriever was brought in one evening very ill indeed and apparently suffering from parvovirus; all the symptoms and that dreadful smell. I admitted her and started fluids at once, but was shocked by the owner's assurance that she had been vaccinated. I asked the owner to go home and bring back the certificate because I had never seen a vaccinated dog contract the disease; we regarded that particular vaccine as virtually 100 per cent effective.

She came back and said that there wasn't a certificate but she had the telephone number of the breeder who had sold her Kirsty. I rang her and was curtly told that it had been a 'homeopathic vaccine'. I equally curtly informed the breeder that there was no such thing as a homeopathic vaccine and did she think it reasonable to sell a pedigree retriever for £900, assuring the purchaser that she 'had been vaccinated' when she manifestly had not? And would she reimburse the client for the fees that were going to be necessary for two days of hospitalisation and drips? I got an insulting answer on the phone and saw that I was wasting my time.

Kirsty did get better; being six months old she may already have had some partial resistance and the bigger they are the easier they are to get onto intravenous fluids and save. The bill was substantial but the owner was happy to pay it. Parvo is also massively contagious so the whole surgery needs to be swabbed out afterwards and any surfaces that the animal touched, disinfected.

There is just one condition, which is not a true infection, that can slightly resemble parvovirus but occurs in fully-grown animals, called haemorrhagic gastroenteritis. It happens more quickly than parvo and it was never clear what sparked it off. Perfectly healthy, vaccinated adult dogs suddenly started passing disgusting, bloody diarrhoea – sometimes virtually pure blood – and its smell did indeed resemble that of parvovirus, but all tests for the virus used to prove negative. It was thought in those days to be some sort of allergic reaction and it did respond dramatically to a combination of antibiotics and steroids. In most infections, steroids are absolutely contra-indicated (that is, out of the question) as they depress the immune system, but since this seemed to be a combination of allergy and auto-infection they got better as fast as they had succumbed.

To return to researchers, a while ago a good friend from Bristol, Graham Betton, who later did his research at Cambridge in oncology, invited me to come over from France for his sixtieth birthday celebrations at Wolfson, his old college. My daughters at that time were very small and I had never left them before. I explained about Graham:

'He's much more clever than daddy, he did a PhD at Cambridge.'

'Does that mean he can do magic tricks?' asked our three-year-old Manon.

At that party I bumped into Professor Neil Gorman, whom I knew vaguely. He had been one of Graham's fellow postgrads and became a pioneer of monoclonal antibody research. I told him that I'd once been to a lecture of his.

'It was one of the specialised immunology seminars at BSAVA Congress.'

'Did you enjoy it?' he enquired, politely.

'Well, I only understood one bit; that was when you stood up and said "Good afternoon".'

Clever people, researchers.

CHAPTER 7

NIGHTS AND WEEKENDS

Night and weekend work, for many practices, has become less onerous since the more recent advent of night-only or 24-hour clinics which have sprung up around the country and to which practicing vets can subscribe. These are not intended to be clinics where the public can turn up for routine vaccination at midnight, but for genuine emergencies. They are expensive as there are two shifts of vets and nurses to cover the whole day and night. But they supply a valuable service and one which the public, used to having A&E open all the time, have come to expect. If one's own practice supplied that sort of service, the fees might almost have to double.

For nights and weekends in Romsey after three years on my own, I had a stroke of luck. I had already approached Ralph Proverbs, as the most logical arrangement would have been for the two Romsey vets who were working alone, to loosely combine for out-of-hours work. Ralph said he would be very interested, but his senior partner entirely vetoed the idea. However, help was to come from an unexpected quarter.

I had got in contact with a vet called David Davies who had an excellent practice in Chandlers Ford, a few miles from Romsey. We went out for lunch and I was going to ask him if he was interested in sharing nights and weekends, but when he told me that he and his partner Norman Neill were perfectly happy with the way things were, I didn't bother even to ask him. But we got on well and it was good to have met him. However, about three weeks later he rang.

'John, was there some sort of question that you were going to ask me?'

'Yes, I was hoping you might be interested in sharing nights and weekends but when you told me about your set-up, I didn't think you'd be interested.'

'Well, I am now. Do you remember I told you that Norman is a besotted sailor in his spare time, has a big catamaran down at Poole, and has done the single-handed Azores race?'

'Yes, I remember thinking what a fantastic hobby.'

'Well, this morning he finished an operation, threw his forceps across the theatre and said "I've had enough, Dave. I want to leave and sail full time".'

'Ah?'

'Well, Norman's the senior partner and owns two-thirds of the practice. I'll have to get a huge bank loan to buy him out and in the meantime, I'm going to work single-handed like you until it's paid off - it's going to take a few years. Are we on?'

We certainly were, and in one fell swoop I had every other night and weekend – after Saturday morning surgery - to myself, which felt as if a huge weight had lifted off my shoulders. Yes, we did have to see more urgent cases when on call, but that didn't matter. The sheer joy of switching the voicemail on when I closed the surgery around 7 pm, one evening in two, was beyond belief. We could go out for the evening or simply luxuriate at home, see friends and have a drink, or go for long walks on Saturday afternoon or Sunday. I could go out jogging without there having to be someone at home by the phone and to bed knowing that I wouldn't be woken up. Bliss. The arrangement between David and I worked perfectly; we saw each other's cases, sent them back to the original practice for any follow-ups, did not 'poach' clients and in all those years he and I never had a misunderstanding. We were both re-invigorated from a full night's sleep several times a week and I'm sure we were better vets for it.

Our governing body, the RCVS was absolutely firm that all veterinary practices had to maintain a 24-hour service, 365 days a year without exception, or make sharing arrangements with other ones. This was sternly enforced and any member of the public complaining that they had not had an answer from a vet they had tried to contact could lead to an investigation. Nevertheless, we all thought that it was reasonable, so long as it was our bona fide, existing clients who rang.

Up until the 1990s most medical GP practices provided the same service for their patients, and although they did have the backup of A&E it was a badge of office for many of them that they would do so. After all, it was they who knew their patients and they were the best to give advice on the phone or agree to see them, rather than a stranger on a deputising service. And for vets it was normal and routine to answer the phone to a familiar voice saying something like, 'I'm so sorry to wake you, Mr. Sampson, but I'm terribly worried ...' We would be straight out of bed and heading for the surgery or the house to see the case. Often, vets are half expecting the call anyway if they hadn't been happy about a serious case that day, so it was our duty and our pleasure.

Except human nature is not always like that. One of the unbelievable RCVS rulings at that time was that ANY member of the public could ring us from Yellow Pages (the old listings for businesses such as practices before internet, into which we were obliged to put our numbers), whether they were existing clients or not and could demand to be seen at any time of night or weekend. So instead of decent people - clients whom we knew - waking us up, it became all too often,

'Yeah, I've got this dog…' Or,

'I haven't used you before, but…' Or even worse,

'Are you open?' (This at 3am).

'Yes, sir, we anxiously await your call at all times because you couldn't be bothered to ring at a reasonable hour and you probably will end up not paying us anyway.' Me, cynical? Well, this is a book of confessions and you need to see the downside, too.

I never found a way of answering the question, 'Are you the night-duty vet?' without sounding self-pitying by having to reply, 'Yes I am, but I was also the day-duty vet yesterday and will be again tomorrow.' Yet, astonishingly, if we refused to see any of these people and they felt litigious (and it's usually folks like those who know their rights very well and have a chip on their shoulder against professional people, that are) they could complain to the RCVS.

And with, at the outset, only their side of the story, the embossed envelope from Belgrave Square could later fall onto the mat and ruin vets' lives for a while. It never happened to me, but I knew two colleagues to whom it did and they both said how worrying it was and how long the investigation lasted. How were they to carry on to their maximum ability and concentrate on their work with that sword of Damocles hanging over them?

We ended up forced to see these wretches who had not bothered to register with a veterinary practice and whose animals often hadn't even been vaccinated. There was also a high possibility that they owed money to other practices. There were no mobile phones, of course, and at that time the only way to filter calls (between real emergencies and casual enquiries) was to give one's private number on the voicemail, with the stipulation that it was purely in the case of emergency.

With that, we could at least protect ourselves a little, while still providing 24-hour cover. British law dictates that you have to register yourself with a medical GP so that the notes may be obtained and the capitation allowance paid to them. As a result, NHS doctors and dentists were quite within their rights to refuse to see someone who was not their patient, but vet practices, being private and with no central registry, did not have that option and were breaking professional law if they did.

As you got older it became more difficult to haul yourself out of a warm bed and it was a far cry from your first emergency calls in the early days as a young vet when you rushed out in the car into the night feeling very brave and important. With my combined practice and home being such a rambling old place, I had to have phone outlets installed in six places altogether; two different parts of the practice, three parts of the house and one down in the garden so that it could be heard and answered everywhere.

And even then, what happened when you were in the toilet, shower or needed to get to the shops? The system had to include a facility for a parallel private number too as well as diversion switching for out-of-hours calls and it took BT three days to install the system – the engineer said it was a one-off and the technical people at HQ had designed it specially for me. Once all the cabling had been installed through the building and underground down to the garden, the large and noisy wall-mounted control box clicked and buzzed like an old telephone exchange. It could probably be done today with a silicon wafer, but it did help avoid all-too-frequent conversations such as this:

'Hello, have you closed yet?'

'We have, yes. The surgery is open from 8am to 7pm on weekdays and 8am to midday on Saturdays.'

'Are you still there though?'

'Yes, but it's 8pm and I'm just leaving.'

'Well, I couldn't ring earlier 'cos I hadn't had me tea. What are your hours, again?'

'8am to 7pm and 8am to midday on Saturday.'

'Hang on I'll get a pen... well... as you're still there can I come in?'

'What's it about?'

'Well, my dog got diarrhoea the other day and it's not much better.'

'Give him nothing to eat at all; just water overnight and come in tomorrow morning.'

'But I'm at work.'

At which point you feel like saying, 'And so am I, still, you stupid man. I had a sandwich for lunch and would like to get home for a hot meal.' But of course, professional people like ourselves would never dream of saying anything like that, would we?

It would be unrealistic to claim that severe emergencies often happened simultaneously though one night I had called a nurse back from home and we were operating on a dog with gastric torsion. This is where the stomach twists around on itself, sometimes taking the spleen with it. This cuts off its own blood supply; it starts going black and you have minutes to open it up and untwist it before there is irreparable damage. The phone rang again and she came back from it saying,

'Now a bitch caesar is on its way in.' I was later delivering those pups and vaguely heard the phone ring yet again. Alison had answered it, and added, '… and … sorry … a cut paw that's bleeding.' In reality, when that sort of thing happened it was so crazy that you just started laughing about it, made more coffee and hoped you might later get an hour or two's sleep before morning surgery started.

Doing a locum in Lymington, on the south coast of England I saw a case during the early afternoon clinic; a likeable client who had noticed that her dog's scrotum was slightly enlarged on one side. I examined him and there was indeed a growth in one of the testicles. These are usually either Sertoli or Interstitial cell tumours or Seminomas, but without histology it is difficult to tell them apart; they are just 'lumps'. Some of them can be benign and others dangerously malignant. But in all cases of cancer there is no justification for delay; none of them disappear spontaneously, some just grow slowly but others will rapidly metastasise through the body and all is lost. Why do so many human cancer patients have to wait for ages for surgery? Why are dogs treated better than they?

In all cases of cancer, vets will operate immediately or tomorrow even if they are booked solid; then it's just a case of working a bit later or giving up your lunch break. I told the client I would operate the next day and would she bring him in at eight-thirty?

'Oh gosh that's tricky; we'll both have to be at work by then, tomorrow.'

'I'll come in at seven-thirty if that's better.'

'We both leave home at seven.'

I had a glance at the appointments book and saw I had a thirty-minute gap before the next clinic. It's a quickish operation if you're experienced and in reply to my question, she said he hadn't eaten since the previous evening (starvation before surgery has to be strictly observed). The poor nurse, who had just finished cleaning up the theatre from the morning ops when I told her I had admitted an urgent case did give me a long hard stare but I said 'pretty please' and 'I'll help you clean up after.' The op was soon over and subsequent histology revealed that it had been one of the malignant ones. And I did help the nurse clear up.

A week later I was eating a salad at lunchtime on a bench down by the Marina and that client came up to me.

'It's Mr. Sampson, isn't it? Thank you so much for doing the operation in your free time, it made all the difference.'

'Is he OK now?'

'Yes, I brought him in for his stitches but I saw one of the other vets.'

'I'm glad he's better.'

'Do you sail at all? We've got a yacht.'

'No, apart from some small boats when I was young – I don't think I've ever set foot on a yacht.'

'Are you free on Sunday?'

'Yes I am.'

'Are you married?'

'No.'

'Have you got a girlfriend?'

'Yes.'

'Well, why don't you both come out with us around the Isle of Wight? We're unashamedly social sailors and the gin and tonics are as important as the fresh air but you'll enjoy it.' So that led to a smashing day out, and all because of a testicle.

So once again the question. Why does it appear - at least on the surface - that animals get better treatment than humans? How could it be that a dog with a testicular tumour was operated on right away but if I were diagnosed with the same thing, I would have to wait months for an operation on the NHS? Why can you ring your vet and get an appointment today but try your GP practice and be told that the first one available is next Thursday? Even with aggressively malignant tumours, if they are diagnosed quickly and surgically removed immediately, there is a chance they may have not yet metastasized (spread). With cancer, delay should not be an option.

Some years ago, we came over to England for a holiday to explore Norfolk and were staying at Wymondham, near Norwich. Our youngest daughter Manon who was then eleven had been complaining of feeling unwell with vague symptoms of sore throat and chest pains. But the day after - a Saturday morning - she said she felt better and we all went off to the local swimming pool. She was a strong swimmer for her age but having done a single length she came out of the water very short of breath, saying she had bad pains in her left upper chest. She described it 'as if there is a sort of string pulling really hard on my heart.'

We were not registered with any GP practice in the UK but had our EU health cards and insurance. In any case, we would have happily paid cash to have been seen privately. But we were shocked to find not only that the local practice, at eleven on a Saturday morning was locked up but there were no notices on the metallic, garage-style door giving surgery times or what to do in emergency.

There was a chemist's shop opposite, who told us to drive to a 'drop-in' NHS clinic in Norwich which remained open all weekend.

Having found it we were amazed that it was packed out on a Saturday afternoon, though probably because of Manon's age we were seen quite quickly. But just by a nurse, who thought it was bronchitis and prescribed her the antibiotic Amoxicillin. She improved a little but still had the heart pains and when we got back to France three days later, she was seen as an emergency within hours of ringing. They immediately ran bloods and found that she had an acute case of the cardiac form of Lyme disease. Before going on holiday to England she had been on a school trip into a forest and one or two of the pupils had found they had picked up ticks when they got home. Manon must have been one of the unlucky ones to have caught an infected tick although we never saw one, nor the 'bulls-eye' radiating reaction around the bite that is regarded as typical. After two weeks of intravenous antibiotics, she recovered and is cured.

So why was the GP practice shut on a Saturday morning without any display of surgery hours and no option of paying someone privately? And when we went to Norwich why was she not seen by a doctor? This is where I return to the idea of scale. Most huge organisations are simply so unwieldy that they cannot be effectively controlled or supervised. I had a friend, Jenny, who went to work for the UN in Geneva and after being there for six months she said on the phone that not only did she do almost nothing in the office all day, they didn't even know what they were supposed to be doing.

Another friend got a job immediately after graduating from Aberystwyth in Glenys Kinnock's Welsh office at the EU in Brussels. He too related that the whole setup was so vast that if he fancied a week off, he just rang in sick and nobody bothered to check.

I was visiting a friend in Southampton General Hospital in the '80s and the one nurse apparently on duty on that ward was rushed off her feet.

'Nurse, could you refill my water jug, please?'

'I won't be long, love.'

'Nurse, my drip has finished and there's blood running down the tube…'

'I'll get to you in a minute.'

'Nurse…'

'I can't come any quicker, love, we're short-staffed.'

The patients were very understanding about this poor nurse trying to deal with a whole ward on her own, but on leaving I missed the 'Exit' sign, turned the wrong way and was apparently walking deeper down that section in a corridor. About to turn back, I heard voices and saw a door ahead of me partly open and some smoke emerging (yes, you were allowed to smoke in hospitals then). I spotted what must have been the nurses' break room and there were about ten of them sitting around with mugs of coffee, smoking and chatting. I don't suggest that this is typical and of course, most NHS nurses do work a hard day and are dedicated to their job and patients, but it really did happen and I offer it as an example of the impossibility of overseeing people at that sort of scale.

In any huge organisation, whether it be the NHS, the education system, government, the BBC, the EU or any other major outfit, there will be a percentage of the staff who almost never ring in sick and work their socks off all day. Another percentage will take frequent days off ill and float through the day trying to keep their heads down. The last fraction will make a career of staying at home whenever possible, doing as little as they can get away with, drawing the salary the State pays them and nobody's the wiser.

This can't happen in a veterinary practice or any small business. The salaries are not paid out of a bottomless government or EU pit; work equals selling your product or providing your service, which leads to money coming into the business and the bills and staff salaries paid. There is no way around it. Although in this account I have painted my own practice as constantly growing, that was true only in a general sense but there were quiet weeks and months particularly early on and during several of them I paid my nurse's salary out of my own savings as there had been no profit in that particular period.

In France it is completely different in the health system as you always pay your GP, specialists and the hospitals directly in cash, by cheque or by credit card. You are then partially reimbursed from your contributory health insurance, where the premiums are automatically deducted from your salary at source. It is a system that really works; the contribution is a reasonable monthly sum and not to be compared with the insurances paid out in the USA, because over there fees, hospitalisation and operation costs have spiralled so far that the most simple and basic medical or surgical interventions now start in the thousands of dollars.

It may also highlight how a totally 'free' system such as the British NHS is its strength as well as its greatest weakness, in terms of any sense of gratitude on the part of patients for what is done for them. GP practices are paid on the number of patients registered with them rather than the number of patients that are seen. Does this give them the incentive to remain open at times that are convenient for the patients? And in human psychology, do we value the things that we get for nothing? I don't think I do. Veterinary practices, to be paid and to be available, have to be open at all reasonable times and the idea that there would not be a Saturday morning surgery would be anathema to us. Ours were always packed, as for some clients working full-time it was often the only slot they could make. The same applied to remaining available until 7pm or beyond.

In France the going rate for medical GPs varies but it's about twenty-five euros for a consultation and forty to fifty euros for referrals to a consultant. You also pay the pharmacy for any prescriptions, again presenting your health card. You will get some of that back and I am convinced that patients respect doctors and hospitals here more for it and are less inclined to waste their time. Equally, if GPs don't see patients face to face they won't earn anything.

In 2023 the Senate will debate the addition of an eighteen-euro fee payable by <u>everybody</u> attending A&E in France except pregnant mothers and infants up to one month of age. I have not met anyone here who thinks this unreasonable as we are all so used to paying modest sums upfront for our healthcare. But just imagine the screams of righteous indignation from opposition MPs if that were proposed in Britain. 'Two-tier health service!!' they would be spluttering and unfair on those who can afford cigarettes, booze and scratch cards but who would be mortally offended if asked to contribute a little to the cost of their doctors. Over there in Britain it's been 'free' for over seventy years and alas has become more a right to be angrily demanded than a unique and incomparable privilege.

It is true that we do pay a bit more for our system than the cost of National Insurance in the UK (for those contributing) but it's slight and those on low salaries pay almost nothing. The system works well, patients are seen quickly and in many cases one can even choose one's surgeon. A friend here who is a stonemason recently had an accident with a power saw and cut so deeply into the cleft between his thumb and first finger that the tendons were severed. It was essential for his work and he made some phone calls, eventually choosing the best surgeon for that kind of injury. He was operated on successfully and now has 95% use of that thumb.

In case you are thinking that I am being a bit harsh on my country of birth and claiming that all is perfect here in 'la belle France', I do admit that there is another side of the coin. Many *'fonctionnaires'* or government employees – over five million of them - in offices up and down the country claim to work very hard when the truth is that some do almost nothing. The French state also guarantees their jobs for life; it is practically impossible for them to be sacked once in post. The lid was taken off this in a hilarious book recently published, by an author who had been employed in many such workplaces, entitled, 'Absolument Débordé!' She saw how much time was wasted, how little was achieved in a day and wrote that however little they did, they would always, when asked, swear that, 'We're rushed off our feet!'

This leads me to my penultimate chapter, on a much more controversial area.

Chapter 8

Bureaucracy

In our work we are lucky that - in contrast to those slaving in our sister profession - there is relatively little bureaucracy. Reading Max Pemberton's excellent book, '*Trust me, I'm a (Junior) Doctor*', we can rejoice in two very important aspects of our work. Firstly, there are very few practices with over ten vets and the rest vary from single-handed to maybe the optimum number of four or five vets, plus the rest of the team.

These numbers allow each vet reasonable night and weekend time off without becoming too bureaucratic or so large that misunderstandings and mistakes often occur. What struck me again and again about Dr. Pemberton's book was the sheer 'creakiness' of such a vast organisation as the NHS. So many employees and the constant poor communication with one doctor or nurse failing to tell the others important things, under the pressure of work. Add to those the demands from senior doctors on one side, colleagues on another, nurses on another, patient demands on yet another, and an army of administrators on the rest.

To say nothing of the urgent need to get out of the hospital (occasionally on time) to buy food, eat and sleep.

The second aspect is the paperwork: patient discharge letters, drug charts and signatures for even a single dose of paracetamol which may involve crossing to a far ward in an outer wing of the hospital if it's at night. There are notes to get up to date, blood requests, biopsy demands, radiology, referrals to and from another ward, obtaining notes and the whole gamut. There have been many initiatives where huge and vastly expensive computer systems have been installed to 'reduce paperwork' and 'improve communication' (oh yes) but most hospital doctors have reported that they have been so poorly designed that they make things worse.

In veterinary practice you are usually in control. There are only as many staff as the practice's financial turnover can afford to employ and sufficiently few that communication errors are rare. You will have the practice dispensary immediately to hand and you prescribe and inject most meds yourself. You often admit cases personally and can therefore explain things to the owners and then later when you discharge them after hospitalization, in a consultation you make sure that the owners are aware of possible complications or relapse problems. No consultants to roar at you and call you a fool in front of the patients, no letters to GPs (because they are you), just the computer records to get up to date and overall, because you are an efficient small unit, it usually runs smoothly. There are emergencies all the time, of course, and a significant part of a vet's day is unexpected, but you are working under conditions where, in general terms, misunderstandings are rare and the work gets done properly.

. . .

The local authorities, of course, were bureaucratic by definition. One day I had a call from Romsey's environmental health department.

'Do you have any clinical waste coming out of your practice?'

'Yes, quite a lot.'

'Well, how do you dispose of it?'

'All the used needles and blades go into sharps boxes and are taken away by a specialist company to be incinerated.'

'Do you have to pay for that?'

'Yes.'

'Any other?'

'Well, we do remove organs and other parts of the body such as in neutering and in the case of tumours and the like. There is also infected material, swabs and dressings.'

'What do you do with all that?'

'We triple-wrap them and they go into the normal household waste.'

'But you should have a special clinical waste arrangement for things like that.'

'Quite agree.'

'Because it just isn't justified to dump them into the household waste.'

'Absolutely.'

'We'll have to start a special clinical waste collection weekly from your premises.'

'That will be fine.'

'You'll have to pay for it, you know.'

'Yes, happy with that.'

'Well, we'll get back to you.'

Nothing happened for a year or more I guess, and then I got a call from a different voice at the same office at

Duttons Road, asking, 'Do you have any clinical waste coming from your practice?' No clinical waste collection was ever instituted during my tenure of the practice. Go figure.

A colleague in Lyndhurst told me he had had a similar approach from New Forest DC. They did start such a collection – at least, sort of. He agreed to their price and was supplied with special yellow clinical waste bags, but was told that they would be picked up on a date different from the normal weekly refuse collection.

The bags needed to be left outside the practice on that specified day and not put into the wheely bins. He complied to the letter with their demands to find that on the first agreed collection date they came the day after, and overnight the bag had been torn open by dogs or foxes and the clinical waste strewn all over the pavement. The second week they arrived a day early and stridently demanded at reception where the bags were. And the third week they didn't come at all, at which point he cancelled the arrangement.

Another time at my practice an inspector arrived and opened with,

'I've come to check your First Aid box.'

'We haven't got one.'

'Well, you're in defiance of the law, sir. All businesses have to have one.'

'OK, let me show you. In this cupboard we keep all the dressings, bandages, splints, orthopaedic instruments, pins and plates. Over there is the dispensary with all the meds, injectables, tablets and capsules. Here are the sterile packs for abdominal surgery, dentistry, suturing and general procedures. That room is the theatre, that one is radiology and the one next to it is the darkroom. Over there is…'

'… Yes, I think I've got the idea.'

'Do you still think I should have a little box on the wall with a cross on it?'

'No sir, thank you for your time.'

We were frequently asked to agree to have school pupils as observers as part of what was called the WEEP scheme; the work experience programme for youngsters. They were usually nice kids, but to be honest a bit of a nuisance and rather got in the way, but we did it as a civic duty and agreed to have several teenagers every year. One year, having been asked as usual, I was sent a letter stating that I would have to insure them. I replied that I was happy that they should be insured but I could see no reason why this should be at my expense.

The administrators apparently had some idea that these teenagers were useful to us and that we should be willing to spend the money, which was the opposite of the case. They then sent me a form to complete, including that they '... *would not be exposed to any hazards whatever*', and if that were to happen it would be our responsibility. We pointed out that in a vet practice there are dogs that bite, cats that scratch, X-rays that can damage DNA and smelly anaesthetic gases that can make you feel woozy. There are infected dressings, sharp things like needles and used scalpel blades and in addition, if one came out on calls with us there were horses and farm animals that also bite and frequently kick. We heard no more and never had students again (except those closer to A levels who applied individually through their parents who were usually clients anyway) which was a pity.

Another friend was a vet who had a post-graduate Fellowship in ENT (ear, nose and throat) surgery. She saw referred cases around Hampshire and the south of

England, returning later to carry out the operations at the practices when necessary. After a while, she grew tired of so much driving and decided to seek planning permission to convert part of the ground floor of her large house in the country into an operating theatre.

This involved knocking two rooms into one to provide a larger space with an examination table, a separate operating table and a section for instruments, autoclaves for sterilising and the rest. She would also convert an adjacent room into a small waiting area, but as all cases were referrals, there would seldom be more than one client waiting at any one time – it was not open to the general public as such. Outline planning consent was agreed and she was beginning the process of getting estimates when she had a call from Hampshire CC environmental health department.

'We don't see a disabled toilet on your plans.'

'There isn't one.'

'But you have to provide one.'

'There is a small downstairs loo that clients would be welcome to use.'

'No, but not specifically for the disabled.'

'It's my own home and I'm not disabled.'

'Then I'm afraid we will have to refuse you planning permission.'

'Couldn't I have a handle bolted to the wall next to the WC?'

'No, there are more aspects than that which will be required. For one it will have to be much bigger to accommodate wheelchairs.'

'But a wheelchair owner couldn't get into my house unaided as there are two quite high steps going up to the entrance door.'

'That's even worse,' she was told. She of course abandoned the project.

The profession is administered by the Royal College of Veterinary Surgeons (RCVS). Their work is important and they deal with all the constitutional and disciplinary aspects of the profession and additionally oversee mandatory CPD ('continuing professional development'). These involve either conferences, weekend refreshers or local update meetings and all the certificate, diploma and Fellowship professional post-graduate exams.

The other principal association is the British Veterinary Association (BVA), among whose roles is to host an annual Congress and to print and distribute the main professional journal, the *Veterinary Record* and virtually all vets become subscribers. Then there is the BSAVA already mentioned, the British Cattle Veterinary Association (BCVA) and the equine branch, the BEVA. In addition, there are various smaller and more specialist organisations and a number of professional newspapers. These mostly involve general articles of interest to vets and nurses plus trade and pharma advertising. To work as a vet in any capacity in the UK or call yourself a veterinary surgeon you have to be a member (MRCVS) or FRCVS. And you pay them a large annual retention fee all the way through your career for the privilege of doing so.

Let me say here that I have never personally been in trouble with the RCVS nor was my membership ever questioned or refused so I have no individual axe to grind. But, essential as their work is, most vets are aware that their monopoly is sometimes abused. They are the centre of the profession but this should not excuse them for some of the past over-reactions, attacks on members and bureaucratic blunders that we used to read about. The annual retention fee – that is, the sum paid annually by every vet working in the UK is (2021 figure) £364 – quite a sum for a young graduate at a time when they may be opening mortgages and starting a family. And they virtually all have to pay, in addition, the subscription to join the BVA (though that is reduced for younger vets) and probably at least one other organization.

The nearest analogous colleges that I can find in human medicine are the RCGP (Royal College of General Practitioners) whose annual retention fees are proportional to the GP's income. For those earning less than £50,000 a year, the fee is £265. The corresponding association for surgeons is the Royal College of Surgeons (RCS), whose annual fees are £316 for the first ten years of membership. Why is subscription to the RCVS higher?

The ever-genial Alastair Porter, who was Registrar of the RCVS for twenty-five years, noted when he retired that at the old premises in Belgrave Square there were 'never more than twenty employees' and the bulk of their work was maintaining the Annual Register. This was 'bashed out on manual typewriters,' he recalled, with everything saved on paper. It was thus very difficult to alter or amend and each time there was a change they had to be re-typed before sending to the printers, bound and posted to the members. Nowadays the Register is virtual, kept on a hard disc or two and any updating should be quick and easy.

There are about 20,000 working vets in the UK and they alone, at that sum, will bring in more than £7 million to the RCVS coffers. How do they manage to spend it? Does the Registrar take the entire staff out to *Le Gavroche* once a week? And that is just the UK vets; in addition, there are legions of members on the foreign, commonwealth and retired lists who pay a lower annual fee to keep their MRCVS. They also earn money payable for entry to exams, certificates, diplomas and Fellowships. I have googled very little to write this book but have had a peek at the RCVS website. They now have over one hundred employees and on the recruitment pages there is not a single photo of them inside the premises at work; they are either taken at receptions and restaurants, or in one case (tantalizingly) at a beach somewhere.

I have just re-googled their recruiting ads and I think I should write this out in full. Their 'Contractual Benefits Package' for employees is the following:

- 33.75 working hours per week.
- Twenty-five days holiday with an additional day added every two years, up to a maximum of thirty days, plus the eight bank holidays.
- Permanent health insurance.
- £250 'well-being' allowance – spend up to £250 on anything linked with well-being.
- £150 Life Assurance – receive £150 for taking out a life assurance policy.
- SMART pension (AEGON – NewGP).

There follow a whopping twenty-five other perks listed under 'Non-Contractual Benefits Package'. Am I exaggerating? Read it for yourselves. Now I see that we don't need to count expensive restaurants into the equation and begin to realise where all the money is going. Remuneration packages, perks, bonuses, handouts and working conditions that vets up and down the country could only dream of, but have to pay for.

Another site shows a 2021 newspaper article where they are claiming that their premises in SW1 are 'no longer fit for purpose' and they must move. What is happening?

Are the ceilings falling in? Are the floors riddled with dry rot or wood-boring beetle? My guess is that the jargon conceals the fact that they have created so many highly-paid new posts that there is no remaining desk space. Are they coming to resemble companies or government departments where the bigger they get, the more they need to grow? In such scenarios, new management levels are created and piled on top of each other; bureaucracy increases exponentially, 'human resources' become an end in themselves and administration departments are created to administrate the administrators.

Has their excellent original mission of having a small, dedicated team to manage and control the veterinary profession been lost to managing and protecting themselves? Nobody argues that the veterinary community does not need to be scrutinised and run properly and high professional standards maintained, but more than a hundred employees for such a small profession? Please.

According to the site, they have an HR department and a 'Chief recruitment officer'. Does that mean that there may be an 'assistant' or 'deputy' one? And if so, do they have a secretary each or do they share one? Committee places are sought-after and for jobs, with a London-weighted salary, an amazingly short working week and all the largesse and bonuses, shouldn't applicants be getting trampled in the rush when a job vacancy crops up? And if the Registrar would interview (or delegate someone to interview) the shortlist, shouldn't that obviate the need for a 'recruitment' department at all?

The annual retention fee has gone up on average just under four per cent a year since 1993 (varying from zero annual increase to twenty-two per cent one year) while the mean rate of inflation averaged out over the same period has been just over two per cent. It's time the RCVS did some practical housekeeping, spent a bit less on itself and reduced the retention fee for young graduates until they are more experienced and earning better salaries. Young vets still start on about thirty thousand pounds (2021) before tax, which may surprise some animal-owners.

Having too many employees can be counter-productive and administrative matters may fall between two stools. Not so long ago we were all delighted to receive an annual retention fee demand arriving in the post in the sum of … zero pounds. Wonderful! A free year at last in recognition of the sums we had been shelling out for so long. But no, another letter arrived later detailing the correct amount due and a brief paragraph that the payment demands had been contracted out to a subsidiary billing company, so it wasn't their fault at all, they claimed. But nobody at headquarters checked them before they went out, did they? And with so many staff on the payroll why did they need to spend money on another company to do their work for them? After this professional negligence, did they refer themselves to their own disciplinary committee?

It is perfectly right that a profession be administered correctly; all vets must read the '*Code to professional conduct for veterinary surgeons*' and there is dead wood in all professions which should be removed. All vets attempt to live up to these maxims but we are human and, whether through fatigue, illness, lack of time or just forgetfulness we can, and do, make mistakes. Indeed, in practice we make them all the time as clinical diagnoses are often no more than educated guesses. We may have family crises, unwell children, personal problems and troubles at home and while these must be relegated to the back of one's mind to concentrate on doing a good day's work, they always nag at you.

You try to understand the question in terms of the general public knowing that in most other professions involving emergency services there are two or even three shifts in 24 hours. In the early Romsey days that I described above, I would work or be on call 24/7 most weeks and on average forty-nine weeks a year. I should not complain about that; it was my choice and if I became chronically sleep-deprived, that was my own fault. But you would at least have hoped that your own governing body would have the imagination to see that you can't keep up that sort of pace without it affecting your judgement.

To go back to the website, I am sure that clinicians up and down the country are soothed that the RCVS has now entered partnership with Stonewall, and delighted that they are now 'fully LGBTQ+ compliant'. (Please don't tell me, though, that there is a gender officer too, or an equal-opportunities one?) I have been unable to obtain even a partial list of the salaried posts at Horseferry Road, and quite how these partnerships enhance the efficiency of staff doing their job is not explained in the blurb, though I bet they mop up time nicely.

Regularly between the 1970s and when I left the profession in 2003, we would read in the veterinary press of practitioners hauled up to London to appear in front of the disciplinary committee for clinical mistakes and errors of judgement, considered by them to amount to 'disgraceful conduct in a professional respect'. The members had the right to instruct lawyers to argue in front of the committees or the RCVS's legal department and some were upheld and those members suspended or struck off - for a fixed period - or otherwise disciplined and in other cases the accusation was quashed. But even in the latter instance it was worrying and expensive for the members involved and the case could last months.

One involved a young farm vet. As I described above, tuberculin testing is a routine procedure necessary in all herds of cattle to reduce the spread of tuberculosis, a chronic debilitating disease that can also pass to humans, so of the greatest importance. But one of the baffling MAFF rules was that no vet was permitted by them to test the herd of a relative. I suppose this was theoretically that it was thought they might cook the results or hide positive reactors. But we all felt that no vet would do that – TB is too serious – and anyway, if they did turn to such an illegal resort, couldn't they equally do it for friends? Most vets are on social terms with their farm clients, so the ruling was ludicrous.

The farms need a bit of notice for testing as each animal has to be injected with a tiny dose of two different types of tuberculin into the side of the neck so you have to get up close. The herd must be contained in runs or stockades so they can be filed through into 'crushes' where the vet can get close enough to inject the minute dose of tuberculin with special syringes just a few millimeters under the skin surface to each animal. Then we went back seventy-two hours later and 'read' the reactions, noting each tag or brand number and recording the results. And finally, back at the practice we do the paperwork and it is sent off to the ministry.

This particular vet's boss had been due to carry out the test but was ill that morning. The test was booked, the herd was enclosed and all was ready, but the problem was that the farmer was the assistant's uncle. Yet he simply had to go ahead with it in those exceptional circumstances. Later he got his employer to sign off the (perfectly genuine and correct) results, and that appeared to be that. But MAFF (which was hurriedly renamed Defra in 2001 straight after the foot-and-mouth scandal) got to hear about it and the poor chap was called up to London and suspended. With a pregnant wife, he could not earn a salary for that period. Yet in all the years I was in practice I never heard of a vet working for MAFF/Defra carpeted for unprofessional conduct. Indeed, a 132-page report by Dr. C.J. Chesney summarising the proceedings of the disciplinary committee up until 2008 made no mention of any salaried member of Defra even being called to appear. They were too well-protected, of course, as the following stories may illustrate.

Rabies is a most serious and fatal disease. It is the subject of important legislation and all vets are acutely aware of it. It is almost invariably terminal in all the warm-blooded animals that can catch it and the same applies to any human being that a rabid animal has bitten, once symptoms have developed. While cases in the USA are sometimes traced back to infected bats, it is endemic (that is, widely present) among the common mammals in many other parts of the world by one biting another. It is therefore the reason that any dogs and cats (principally) that were coming into the UK from certain countries, had to be quarantined for six months. This is because the virus is capable of lingering in the body for months (very occasionally, up to a year) without causing symptoms and can then explode into the full-blown disease.

MAFF quite rightly took the disease very seriously; we were called to meetings about their 'Rabies Awareness Plan' and were sent extensive literature about the measures that would be necessary if a case were discovered. Any vet who suspected, even vaguely, that an animal exhibiting peculiar nervous symptoms that did not fit in with a known neurological syndrome, most particularly if it was connected with quarantine, was to notify MAFF immediately and a pre-planned investigation process (they claimed) would be set in place.

I had already had one suspected case. Romsey is not far from Southampton which is a port, and there are marinas all along the south coast. Any of those could harbour animals illegally smuggled over in yachts to avoid the cost of quarantine and we were always vigilant. One dog was brought in that had become suddenly viciously aggressive and had bitten its owner and two other family members. No quarantine had been involved but it was dangerous so I had to euthanise it immediately - with difficulty - and then rang MAFF.

In the laboratory, rabies is a difficult disease to prove, but in most cases there are specific 'viral inclusion bodies' seen in parts of the brain when histology is done (examining stained sections of tissue under a microscope). MAFF told me they would have to examine the brain of the dog, so I would need to remove its head. I agreed to that and asked them to come and collect the head as it was not exactly something one could put in the post. They said they had no vans available or any personnel free to come over, so I had no choice but to drive it to Itchen Abbas near Winchester, myself. There had previously been a rather unpleasant rabies vaccine for humans which had to be given multiply into the abdomen, but a better vaccine had just been developed. I had been bitten during the euthanasia but had already had the vaccine, and the two family members who were involved were quickly inoculated. In the event, the result came back negative which was a relief for us as few vaccines are a hundred per cent effective.

But the other case in my practice experience was to show MAFF in quite another light and prove the worst case of overt animal neglect I had ever encountered. New clients came in with a Rhodesian Ridgeback bitch who had just left quarantine. The family had come to England having lost their farm in Zimbabwe to President Mugabe's thugs, bringing almost no money or possessions except Elsa, their treasured friend. She appeared weak and distant; we lifted her between us up onto the examination table (they are a heavy breed) and immediately I noticed that she had a pronounced 'tic'; a 'twitch' involving primarily her face and to an extent the rest of her body. She was not in any way aggressive, indeed the opposite; she was dull and unresponsive. She had completed the mandatory six months quarantine, using up most of her owners' remaining funds and had come out seeming reasonably well. But within a month she had started this weird twitch, and the owners said she was 'depressed and just not herself'.

I went through in my mind the notes from Dr. Penny's neurology lectures at Bristol. Could it be a rare case of the dumb form of rabies? Rabies occurs in one of two principal forms: the 'furious' type (usually in dogs, cats, foxes and other mammals) and the 'dumb' form, most commonly in humans but not totally unknown in animals. Dr. Penny had worked in Kenya where he had seen several rabid dogs and described the peculiar, 'lolloping' kind of walk that they demonstrated. He also described their worried, fixed expressions as they focused on their objectives and moved in very straight lines towards them, with none of the playful, tail-wagging, looking-for-food actions of normal dogs. He said they could become so irrational that if they got to a brick wall, instead of skirting around it, they might try to 'bite their way through it'. He had described seeing one such dog walking straight down a road towards a village where he was working and the local people, knowing exactly what it was, scattering in panic.

In the dumb form, there is no aggression and muscle paralysis develops slowly. One of the muscular reflexes involved at an early stage is the 'deglutition' (swallowing) mechanism. This can become paralysed and affected people, being thirsty, try to drink but the reflex fails and the water goes down into their trachea and lungs, hence coughing and distress. This deteriorates to the point where even the appearance of water makes them gag and they cannot stand the sight of it, hence its other name 'hydrophobia'. Knowing that (extremely rarely) dogs could have the dumb form where paralysis slowly engulfs the whole body and Elsa was clearly ill, as required by the law I rang the ministry at Itchen Abbas. I described the picture at length to whomever I was speaking to (unfortunately I forgot to ask his name), who said,

'I doubt if it's rabies.'

'Well, what else could it be?'

'You're the practitioner, you work it out.'

'She has just come out of quarantine.'

'Yes, but it really doesn't sound like it to me.'

'Could a senior ministry vet come down here to examine her and give me a second opinion?'

'No, we're short-staffed and no one's available.' (Why did they always say that?)

'For heaven's sake, rabies is a legally notifiable disease. This is why I'm notifying you, as I must by law, and I don't think that saying over the phone that it "probably isn't rabies" is good enough. If this does turn out to be rabies and I hadn't notified you, you will be trying to get me struck off.' He seemed to be speaking to someone else and then said,

'OK, we'll send a van and get her brought up here.'

The van arrived, she was put into a steel cage, a tearful goodbye from the owners who had only recently got her back, and she left. I expected a call at least daily from the ministry but heard nothing, so tried ringing them. The ministry buildings were extensive (I'd been up there for meetings) and I had no idea into which section she had gone. The van driver before leaving had not been able to tell me anything and I didn't know who was dealing with her case so I was shunted from department to department with nobody knowing anything about it. Eventually a voice said, 'No, we don't think it's rabies, but we'll keep her a bit longer.' What exactly were they doing? Finally, on maybe my seventh call, with the owners ringing me daily, I got someone again.

'They're sure it's not rabies, they're sending her home.'
'Who is "they"?'
'The people who have been dealing with her.'
'Can you tell me who you are …?' CLICK.

I rang the owners to say that she was on her way back, they arrived expectantly and then it happened. The white MAFF van drove in and Elsa was lying collapsed in the bottom of the same cage, immobile. She was covered in her own diarrhoea and urine and she was moribund. We lifted her out of it and placed her on a blanket. She could not raise her head, her joints were stiff, she was thin, apparently paralysed, dehydrated and on the verge of death. The owners broke down uncontrollably at the sight of her and I left them with her for a minute to run and catch the driver before he sped off.

I interrogated him about who up there had been dealing with her, but he was frightened and said he knew nothing. I asked who had told him to bring her back and he replied that he thought it was a secretary but explained that he was only the odd-job man and driver and it was not his fault. He left and I went back into the consulting room.

'Please put her to sleep, Mr. Sampson; we can't bear to see her go through this.' I did as they wished - it took only a few drops of pentobarbitone - and as we watched her body freed of the suffering she must have endured, I told them,

'I shouldn't say this to you, but I am so furious that I wouldn't blame you for taking the ministry to court over this and I would testify on your behalf.'

'But it won't bring Elsa back, will it?'

'No.' They went outside, talked and she came back in.

'My husband has found a job and we have taken out a mortgage on a small cottage in the country with a garden. We'd like to bury Elsa there.'

I told them that there was no charge of any sort on my practice's part and that I was terribly, terribly sorry. They left and I never saw them again. I had no phone call from MAFF about it, nor any written report or communication and it proved impossible to track down whom or which department had been responsible for this tragic case. I could not prove it but I was convinced that Elsa had not been taken out of that cage for the nine days that she was away.

She almost certainly died of the dumb form of rabies but only a post-mortem and histology of brain tissue could have confirmed that diagnosis. She had bitten no one either at the surgery or in the owners' home so human life had not been threatened, but whoever at the ministry had been guilty of this appalling professional neglect and animal cruelty should have been struck off; not for a year, but for life.

. . .

The mismanagement of the foot-and-mouth epidemic in 2001 was another chilling example of where MAFF, who may have been good at complying with laws, could make a mess of things where real animal welfare was concerned. I was not connected with the measures that were put in place by them during that outbreak, but the experienced reporter Christopher Booker, in collaboration with the epidemiologist Dr. Richard North investigated the epidemic in detail for the magazine Private Eye. Booker also wrote about it in the Daily Mail and the Sunday Telegraph. They concluded that the most appalling blunders had been involved as over seven million cattle, sheep and pigs were shot and carcasses burned the length and breadth of the country.

Private Eye had been involved in so many libel suits in the past that they had become scrupulous in their checking of facts before publication. The whole story was published in a special edition of the magazine in November 2001 and pointed to catastrophic miscalculations on the part of the ministry. They were described in the report as '... *one of the most bloody, tragic and disgraceful misjudgments ever committed in the name of science.*'

It cost the country £2.5 billion, to say nothing of the permanent loss of pedigree herds, bankruptcies and suicides. Plus an estimated £20 billion to the wider economy. The far better alternative of 'ring vaccination' of herds in contact or in the near vicinity, was rejected because the powerful National Farmers Union (NFU) president, was set against it. Doing it that way may have only cost £200 million, less than one percent of the eventual bill. Millions of animal lives and hundreds of livelihoods would have been saved, but that was politics. PM Tony

Blair instigated three separate enquiries (all *in camera*) designed to 'disguise the real truths and protect MAFF'.

> 'The charade of Blair's three "pseudo-enquiries" was shown up when in October 2001, Devon County Council staged an enquiry of its own, under Professor Ian Mercer. This heard five days of devastating evidence from farmers, vets, the local NFU and the RSPCA on all the issues Blair would try to sweep under the carpet. MAFF's total incompetence, wholesale cruelty to animals, the bullying of farmers and vets and the mediaeval barbarity of the contiguous cull policy was … scarcely credible'.
>
> — PRIVATE EYE, NOVEMBER 2001 (P. 30)

Ministry officials were witnessed not complying with their own hygiene regulations, not always changing protective clothing between farms and allowing lorries carrying carcasses to drive through roads in unaffected areas 'dripping blood'. At one farm where it had proved impossible to stockade the herd, the army who had been drafted in were seen going around the fields shooting the cattle at random with rifles. The report surmised that if anyone else had been considered guilty of these actions, MAFF would have been the first to rush to court to prosecute them. Their hypocrisy from February to October 2001 was described as 'unpardonable' as they sought to place all the blame on the farmers.

There was no suggestion that Private Eye was exaggerating the seriousness of the mishandling for journalistic or commercial benefit, and I have a personal letter from a past RCVS President confirming that their report was 'pretty accurate'. Yet I never heard of any ministry vet suspended or removed from the register as a result. Once again, the RCVS and the ministry were too close to each other ('arse and underpants', as George O'Malley used to put it). They were politicians, after all, and across the world they look after their own and know how to watch their backs.

Would someone explain to me the difference between one vet making an administrative error when a signature was substituted (and he being suspended though no animal suffered), and where nobody was apparently blamed after 7.7 million farm animals were slaughtered, the countryside polluted and many farms put out of business? Or putting it another way, why was there one rule for vets in practice and another for vets employed by the State?

One last example of badly-considered legislation was the instance of the new 'pet passport' scheme, though I will say that this was not entirely Defra's fault, as EU legislation is complicated, difficult to interpret and HM Customs and Excise can be very heavy-handed. As more and more British animal owners bought holiday properties abroad (a lot here in France) it was quite understandable that they wanted to share their family vacations with their pets. Kenneling is expensive, the animals frequently pined for their owners and what was more natural than taking their pets abroad with them so they could have a holiday too? Quarantine was by then no longer necessary in those conditions and legislation was developed that in the most part was logical and easily observed. All animals were to be microchipped, wormed, vaccinated against rabies and their pet passports and certificates signed by their vets. The small sticking point was the use of 'worming' drugs such as praziquantel.

The background here is that there are two main forms of intestinal worm infection that domestic animals can contract, and they are both potentially harmful to humans. The first are 'roundworms' such as Toxocara canis and Toxocara cati which can cause blindness in young children if they have accidentally transferred soiled material to their mouths from infected pets. For some reason, this is not included in pet passport legislation but all responsible owners regularly 'worm' their animals against these anyway.

The second is a type of tapeworm, Echinococcus multilocularis, which dogs can pick up from other dogs' droppings. There is a lot of it in underdeveloped parts of the world, though much less in Europe, yet since it also can transmit to human beings it must be treated. Praziquantel is an excellent broad-spectrum anthelmintic, so it should eliminate both roundworms and tapeworms.

The (pre-Brexit) pet passport legislation stated that all dogs or cats who were leaving and re-entering Britain on holiday should be dosed with it (or a similar worming drug) *'not less than 24 hours before travelling and not more than 120 hours (5 days) after.'* This had to either be done personally by a vet or at least the dosing by the client witnessed on surgery premises. Then the vet or an RVN nurse signed it off with the date, time and the practice stamp.

The 'not less than 24-hour' rule was perfectly rational in order to give the wormer time to take effect, but not the 'no more than five days' instruction, since what they completely forgot to take into account was the length and frequency of the stays. Some owners went over on holiday just once or twice a year, while others at work crossed on many weekends in the summer, sometimes for longer spells and maybe less frequent trips over in the winter to check on their properties, each time taking their dogs.

Family came to stay with us for a three-day weekend with their Basset hound, Louis. He was microchipped and up to date with all his vaccinations including rabies and they had their UK practice's signature with the date and time that he had been dosed on a Wednesday lunchtime – the only time they could get to the surgery - before they left. They took the night ferry from Portsmouth the following day (Thursday) and arrived in Le Havre the next morning. They mentioned to us that they had been surprised that they had not been pet-checked at Portsmouth (Louis stayed quietly in the car for the crossing) but assumed that only a percentage of the 'passports' got noted and examined. As a result, they were not asked when they would be returning.

After a lovely weekend with them, they left on Sunday afternoon for the four pm return sailing but rang in distress from Le Havre to say that they had been refused entry by Customs onto the ferry. The inspector had looked at Louis' pet passport and told them that it was over 120 hours since he had had the wormer (by about three hours) and he could not enter the vessel. They drove the fifty kilometers back to us and stayed the night.

They had already missed a day's work by Monday, and I took them to a vet I know here who happily dosed Louis for nothing and stamped the passport. I could have done it myself but by then I was no longer MRCVS (hmmm!). The vet Jean-Marc also commented on how other British clients of his had come unstuck in the same way and how ludicrous he thought the legislation was. In the event, they only lost their salaries for one day each and had to pay forty euros to have their return ticket changed. But others would have had to add the cost of a night's stay in a hotel with a dog (or sleep in the car) and the inconvenience of finding a vet the next day who was not their own, somewhere in Le Havre.

It also begged the question of whether dosing with praziquantel or any other wormer every week is really in the best interests of the dogs or cats. Jean-Marc told me the story of British clients he saw regularly, with two boisterous Dalmatians. They were, as we say here, '*d'un certain âge*', their children had grown up and the dogs were the centre of their lives. They never went anywhere without them and, they said, they helped them to keep fit with all the exercise the dogs needed. They went out with them at least twice a day not only on nice warm days but in bitter or wet weather too, when they probably would have preferred to stay at home by the fire. They spoke quite good French, he said, and had bought a small house which they were slowly renovating and extending with a view to retiring to France in a few years' time, with the dogs of course. They explained to him that they were both in pre-retirement and being given extra time off work, so they would be increasingly coming over for whole weeks rather than weekends as their retirement approached, to finish restoring the house. You can buy a small timber-framed 'maison normande' with work needed, in a picturesque country area for less than a hundred thousand euros around here, so why not? That meant that instead of just being wormed by their UK vet they needed to come to him as well (if over five days later) for a second dose.

Jean-Marc even remarked that in some cases he had signed the certificates <u>without</u> giving the drug because he knew he had dosed them so frequently in recent months that he didn't consider that overdosing was in the animals' best interests. All practising vets would put animal health before poorly-drafted legislation.

. . .

No account of infuriating bureaucracy would be complete without a more light-hearted story (to show that the committee members are human really) and mention of one of the profession's most celebrated eccentrics: the 'Flying Vet'. We were at our newcomers' Centaur (Vet) Society Dinner Dance at Senate House; nervous at our first of such grand functions we were having drinks around the first-year table in the large bar before the meal when I happened to look across to the final-year one. A big bloke stood up, lurched, tried to steady himself and then fell right on top of the table, wiping all the drinks off onto the surrounding dinner jackets and ball dresses. He laughed, cleared it up and went to the bar to buy replacement drinks for them all and seemed to remain as popular with them after as before. I asked someone who he was, and the reply was 'Maurice Kirk'.

A qualified pilot and mostly as a result of escapades with light aircraft all over the world, Maurice got himself into all sorts of scrapes and had a few spells in the nick. The RCVS tried repeatedly to get him stuck off but he knew professional law backwards, virtually always represented himself at the hearings and ran rings around them. Even when the committee pronounced against him, he just took it to the Appeal Court or the House of Lords and usually got away with it. It must not have been fun to have been at the receiving end of some of his more picaresque pranks and there may be ex-members of the disciplinary committee who still wake up at night in a cold sweat after nightmares about him, but he was (and still is, at the time of writing) an unforgettable character and all professions need them.

. . .

To summarise, just as patients used to joke that they didn't make an appointment with their own GP first thing in the morning 'before his stethoscope has warmed up,' at the other end of the day I would advise clients something similar. To anyone I knew well, I would say don't make an appointment to see me after six pm. Especially if I'd been up in the night, I'd be running on empty by that time and that's when mistakes and misjudgments happen.

If you <u>intentionally</u> neglect an animal or your attitude towards your staff or clients was '*disgraceful in a professional respect*', you deserved to be summoned to London to answer for it. That is clear. But the RCVS (in those days anyway, and I'm trying to be scrupulously fair here) seemed to have difficulty distinguishing between that and a member unwittingly making a serious clinical or administrative error. I hope that is a reasonable statement.

To attain the resplendency of a place on an RCVS committee was regarded as a political feather in one's cap and the surest route towards high office and even the Presidency. Automatically, this precluded most members who worked full-time in practice and the committees seemed to comprise mostly academics, government vets and anyone else who had the leisure (or could get paid leave) to travel to London on weekdays, to sit on these prestigious committees. As a result, GPs were under-represented on the disciplinary committee, which was an irony as they are by far the bulk of the profession. Assuming majority decisions, it would have been difficult for any general practitioner on the committee to stick up for a colleague who, in their view, had committed an act that was plainly the result of being exhausted and they could be overruled by other committee members, most of whom were never pulled out of their beds at night or on call all weekend. However, reading more recent literature, it seems that the RCVS has since questioned the severity of its own procedures and committee structure, and that can only be a good thing.

If I have been unbalanced in my critique of both the RCVS and MAFF/Defra in these pages I regret it, but my comments are a product of their time. I have had no contact with the profession in Britain since 2003 when I resigned my membership and have recorded events as faithfully as I can remember them. But they are in the past and my memory is not infallible. Both bodies do important work and I am confident that their attitude towards the vets working under the strenuous conditions of general practice today is more enlightened.

CHAPTER 9

THE END OF LIFE

'Euthanasia' comes from 'eu', the Greek for 'good' as in 'euphoria' and 'euphemism', and the Greek god of death Thanatos, and therefore means 'a good death'. One of the saddest things for us pet owners is the shortness of our loved pets' lives contrasted with our own allotted span; many of us have to endure their deaths five or more times in our lives.

Euthanising a healthy animal is inexcusable except in the most extreme circumstances, but doing so for an old, sick animal where everything has been tried and no hope is left, is the most compassionate act any vet can perform for the animals in their care. Done properly (and we get very skilled at it), it's a quiet, painless intravenous overdose of a barbiturate. The animal feels no distress, loses consciousness and sinks down; wherever possible, in its owner's arms. Some owners did not want to be present at this last act and that was their choice. But in most cases I could persuade them that for the sake of the final moments of their pet, they should hold them and keep on talking to them so the last thing they heard was the sound of their adored owner's voice. I am not naturally emotional, but writing these lines does still make me quite upset, because I can still picture some of the good clients I knew and respected, in floods of tears.

I would refuse point-blank any request for euthanasia for a healthy animal; my nurses got to know the owners well and kept a list of people looking to take on a re-homed animal. If it was a question of leaving the country or moving to where pets weren't allowed, they were very good and could usually, given a few weeks, help to re-home.

A huge skinhead guy came in carrying a lovely white Angora rabbit with a nasty-looking small son who was scowling at me as he wiped his nose on his sleeve.

'I bought this rabbit – cost a fortune – for this little git' (there was apparently no love lost between him and his little prince) 'and he promised to look a'ter it, clean it an'all that but he doesn't touch it so I want you to put it down.' I looked at him, then at the pretty little rabbit snuffling happily on the table, thought about it and said,

'To be honest, I think this rabbit has got as much right to live as he has.' (Indicating his son). For a second daddy's eyes flashed as the vet insulted his little prodigy, but then,

'Do you hear what the doc says, you little sod? You take it home and if you don't look a'ter it, no more pocket money for you ever!' They went off and I never saw them again.

Euthanasia in horses, pigs, sheep and cattle is a different matter as in many cases the farmers want to be able to send the carcasses off for animal feed via what they called the 'knackers' and if chemical methods of euthanasia are used, they can be dangerous if the meat is eaten by other animals. I once saw a beagle belonging to the local Hunt that was brought in staggering around; it could have been a number of things but I admitted him for observation. Within a few hours he was quite normal again, so my guess was that he had eaten some knackers' meat that had contained the euthanasia drug which is not serious in lower doses and resembles sedation.

We had had one single lecture at Langford about the techniques of destroying large animals using a gun; the correct spot to place the barrel on the forehead, the exact angle to fire and the other safety precautions necessary. When I set up my practice, I bought a second-hand Webley Scott .32 automatic pistol with a box of ammunition, notified the police and an inspection was done. What we hadn't had at Langford was any ballistics training though, and I was too embarrassed to admit that to the police firearms officer. Soon after, I had a call from them to a road accident on the Romsey bypass; a young heifer had escaped from a field and had been hit by a lorry. She was in a bad state; terminally injured but still just alive and lowing pathetically.

I drove back to the surgery and returned with the gun, put two rounds into the clip, placed the barrel on her forehead and … click. I checked the clip and tried again … click. The farmer had by that time arrived so I explained that the weapon was malfunctioning and what did he plan to do with the carcass? To my relief he saw that she was too badly injured to pass on down the chain, so he said he would come back with a tractor and forklift to take her to the farm to bury in a field. That meant I could euthanise her any way I wanted, and did so with several bottles of barbiturate.

I took the gun the next week to a dealer in rifles, hunting guns and the like. He looked at it carefully, said it seemed fine and then he smartly pulled back the breech, released it and it sprung back into place, 'Ah … THAT'S what you have to do,' I thought to myself. It's necessary in order to get the first round into the chamber, but I just didn't know. I felt very stupid about it, but the incident passed and over the years in Romsey I had to use the gun many times. In one horrifying case first thing in the morning, I had to destroy a horse that I had gelded the day before and he was one extremely rare case where the intestines had ruptured out of the gelding incision and the poor creature was standing on his own entrails, down in the straw. He must have been in the worst kind of agony and memories like that still give me bad nights from time to time. We didn't usually stitch the wound, to give better drainage. Should I have done so in that case? Was I negligent?

It is tempting to draw comparisons with euthanasia in us humans, but it is a hugely controversial matter with strong feelings on both sides. I hope that the reader will forgive these occasional sallies into the human sphere but we're all animals (well, we're not plants) and I hope it makes sense to occasionally talk about the two in parallel. I am much older than my French wife and I have asked her to promise that if I go completely gaga, I am to have a big sign in heavy felt pen pinned to the end of my home or hospital bed, 'NIL BY MOUTH. DO NOT RESUSCITATE'. Anne says she hates thinking about it and won't give me a straight yes or no answer, but I am determined.

Maybe having seen so much euthanasia, vets are more pragmatic about it. To spare people the really awful bit in the period before death; maybe the acute pain and sometimes the shame and embarrassment, that we do for animals seems natural to us. It remains anathema to many doctors and is forbidden by the laws of the land, except where one does no more than quietly switch off machinery.

My mum was a lifelong non-smoker, but like many in the nineteen-forties and fifties my dad had smoked and later my step-father almost chain-smoked so there was little doubt where it had come from when she was diagnosed with terminal lung cancer. A month before she died, I was visiting her in hospital and she looked absolutely wretched. She gazed at me beseechingly and said, 'John, you've got the drugs, can't you end this for me?' I thought about it very seriously and knew that, yes, I could have given her a small injection or tablets to swallow and I would have ended her suffering, but I would be killing my own mother, however close to death she was at the time. And if found doing so, I could have gone to prison for murder.

That evening I was at a committee meeting about something non-medical and one of the Romsey GPs, a good friend, was present so I asked his advice. He said to go and see the consultant on that ward; they are used to such requests and they will take care of it. I did so but either I caught the consultant on a bad day, or perhaps he was violently against such a suggestion. He described it as 'illegal and out of the question'.

Ultimately it was down to a locum GP. At her request, we had brought mum back to die at home but in the upheaval of that, the promised diamorphine pump which she should have had was overlooked. In those cases, one can simply override it as two of my friends have said they quietly did at home with a loved one at the very end. We had made a temporary bedroom for her in the front downstairs room, and on the first night home she started waking from her heavy sedation and became extremely distressed. We called the locum service, he arrived, looked around the room and commented, 'It hasn't changed much'; it appeared he had lived in that house in the past. Giving her a large injection, he declared, 'We treat the patients in these cases, not the families.' Within minutes of his leaving, it was over.

To the comment above about 'Nil by mouth', although Anne does not agree, for me it is a very logical and rational request. Finishing this in 2022, I am seventy-five, fit as a fiddle, hope to get to my nineties in pretty good shape and, most importantly, remain useful. I have not the slightest fear of death when it arrives, but dread the idea that I could be conscious yet imprisoned in a permanently useless body that will never recover. Or that my brain might go and I can no longer make any decisions. Death would then not be 'euthanasia' but 'dysthanasia' - an awful death. Why should my useless body block up a hospital bed when it could be available to make someone better and go home? This is why it is such a privilege for vets to quietly put an animal 'to sleep' when all hope is gone and before those last, unbearable weeks or months. The sooner it is acceptable by British (and French) law for humans - rather than having to travel to a flat in Switzerland - the better.

Disposal of bodies when the owners do not want to take them home for burial is a big headache for vets and wherever possible we try to persuade owners to find a way of naturally burying their pets. There are professional pet cemeteries with return of the ashes but they are very expensive. In other cases, vet practices in cooperation with the local authorities have to find facilities for mass burial or incineration, but it really is not an area that vets want to be involved in and yet have to be.

We had a large chest freezer for animals brought in dead or euthanised, and the cadavers were for a while taken away once a week by what described itself as a 'professional incineration' company. Alas, a national newspaper investigated the company and we were shocked to discover that some of the animals were being skinned. Of course, we immediately stopped using (and paying) them, but what to do with the bodies? I repeat that we did our best to persuade owners to arrange for burial or pay the quite high charges for individual cremation, but many clients could not do so or pay the extra. It remains a big problem for practices.

Some clients asked for the pet to be quietly put to sleep at home. One such was an amusing chap and long-standing client called Tony Bryson, who utterly adored his old black Labrador. He had explained to me that the dog had stuck by his side during some difficult personal times and was like his oldest friend. I had already had to operate on him several times including removing most of his teeth and one of his eyes with an ocular tumour, and he playfully called him 'Frankenstein'. The dog became very senile and unsteady and when the decision was made, he asked me to go up to his house. He also requested me not to bring a nurse to help with raising the vein so I went alone and found him out in the garden next to the deep hole that he had dug, with one arm around the dog and the other hand holding half a bottle of scotch. Under my instruction, he raised the vein and in seconds it was over. He didn't want my help to put him into the grave and said he just wanted me to leave and have a few more moments alone with his old pal. Few memories can be more poignant.

A client had two beautiful English Setters who were whisked to me immediately if there was ever the slightest trouble and she had once or twice come to the surgery accompanied by teenage foreign students. She explained that as a commercial venture she took in these students who were over for English language classes, giving them bed and breakfast with an evening meal and a packed lunch to take with them to their language schools. She had recently gone from having one student up to three and had bought extra bedroom furniture for them, second hand.

One day one of the Swedish girl students had tiny bites on her face and arms. She took her to her GP who referred her to a dermatologist, who diagnosed an infection with Cheyletiella parasitivorax, a parasite similar to a louse that is quite common in animals and can transmit to humans. I examined both dogs under a powerful illuminated lens and could see no sign of any such infection, and Setters' coats are always so silky that you can usually see beasties that should not be there. As a precaution, however, the nurses soaked them in an insecticidal wash called Alugan, which is very effective and is then left to dry on the animal to leave traces for extended protection.

They went home and all seemed well but she came back a week later and said a new German girl had now developed a similar rash. We had the dogs back and tried a different anti-parasitic shampoo but all the way through I had been convinced that the dogs were not the culprits. Yet she repeated that the dermatologist was quite firm; that was the diagnosis and the dogs were the source. Then one Sunday morning she rang in a hysterical state.

'Mr. Sampson, the German girl has been admitted to the dermatology ward of the Royal South Hants as an urgent case because she woke up this morning with her face and one arm covered in marks. I'm terrified that she is going to be scarred for life and I want you to put the dogs down.'

'No, I can't do that… but just a minute, did you say she woke up like it?'

'Yes.'

'So, she was fine when she went to bed.'

'Yes.'

'And no contact with the Setters overnight?'

'No, none.'

'Is she sleeping in the same bed that the previous Swedish girl used?'

'Let me see... er... yes.'

'I'm coming over to the house. I've got something happening here at the moment but I'll be there in an hour.'

In the event I didn't have to go; I had realised what the problem almost certainly was and she rang me half an hour later to say there was no need to come. They had looked at the girl's bed and seen two small flat creatures on the sheet. Bed bugs. They then examined the wooden joints of the second-hand beds they had bought and found that there were more. The wretched things only come out at night when they detect the warmth of a body in the bed, feed on skin debris, thus causing a rash and are seldom seen in the daytime. The student got better without scarring, the bunks were burned and that was the end of the tale.

Euthanasia while under anaesthetic in some cases is a routine part of a vet's day and it once again highlights what veterinary surgeons are allowed to do, in contrast to our human equivalents. Many, particularly older, animals can present with vague abdominal symptoms; some pain to the touch, some swelling and perhaps off their food, a potent sign that all is not well. We take radiographs and run blood samples but often the radiographs are difficult to interpret and such an animal can have a fairly normal blood picture. In those cases, the answer is, again, an exploratory laparotomy, to open up the abdomen and have a good look around. Much of this is now done as 'laparoscopy' using fibre-optic equipment but that equipment was in its infancy then and, before mass production, expensive to buy.

Three advantages of the old-fashioned method were: first, that the operation can be carried out through a midline incision (the animals on their backs on the table) which involves very little cutting to access directly into the abdomen and with a minimum of suturing at the end. Secondly, with fibre-optics it is often difficult to get the probes to pass easily through the abdomen and things may be missed. With a laparotomy the entire abdomen is there in front of your eyes, or at least to the touch of your fingers and the third advantage is that it is also much quicker. With so many organs involved (stomach, intestine, liver, spleen, kidneys, ureters, bladder, adrenals, lymph nodes - and ovaries and a uterus in some cases) there are so many things that can go wrong.

This is not a pathology textbook so I won't name them here but one very obvious possibility in old animals is cancer within the abdomen, which can start in any of the organs mentioned. Some may be single and involve just one organ or part of it and discrete tumours involving the stomach or intestines can be removed by resection. A small missing part of the intestine is of no consequence as it is so long; ditto removing a discrete stomach tumour. The liver is a very delicate structure and cancer removal is more complicated. The same applies to most of the other essential organs, though the spleen may be removed entirely without too serious an effect on the animal. In too many cases though, we are faced with multiple tumours or those that have 'seeded' throughout the abdomen, that is, where cells from the primary growth have become detached, cross the abdomen and start to grow everywhere.

When faced with this or any other completely inoperable condition, the question is, 'Is it right to close the incision and let the animal come round, with a hopeless prognosis and a short time to live?' In every case, I would

The End of Life

stop and ring the owners (or in some cases they had actually asked to stay in their car or in the waiting room). I would explain the situation and recommend that their pet should not be allowed to come out of anaesthesia, which was then deepened until death intervened. It was the owners' final choice but no client I knew ever asked for them to be allowed to recover, all recognising that the last stages would be harrowing for loved pet and themselves equally.

A particularly searing case that almost broke my heart involved one of the loveliest old couples I ever met as a vet. I have already mentioned the clients that we looked forward to seeing and who could really make our day. These were a classic example and they had two Siamese cats, one very ancient and the other middle-aged. The couple used to come straight to the surgery if the slightest thing was wrong with them. Money was no object; they were always funny and occasionally had so much to say to each other that they seemed to forget I was around, with little asides and mutually-shared giggles. But then on a certain day it all changed. He rang one evening.

'Mr. Sampson, I want you to put the cats to sleep.'

'What has happened?'

'It's my wife... she has died. She had a heart attack.'

'Oh, I'm so sorry, I can't believe it... when?'

'Yesterday.' Of course; he was in shock and over-reacting, I reasoned.

'But you love the cats so much.'

'Yes, I do but I'm going to have to sell the house and go into a home and they won't take animals.' I realised that he couldn't possibly have established all that, just one day after his wife's death.

'Look, you're in bereavement, you have a lot to think about and you must organize the funeral. Can I help with that? Don't worry about the cats; we'll have them here and my nurses will be able to re-home them if it comes to it.'

I heard no more from him for three days but he arrived without an appointment on a very busy evening surgery, asking me again to euthanise the two cats. I wish I had had more time with him but was already running critically late with appointments and the waiting room was almost full. I talked to him about the options but he was absolutely adamant,

'You must put them to sleep; it's my request.' He became terribly agitated, wept and in the end, against everything that I held right, I complied with his wishes. He asked how much he owed us. I replied,

'Nothing. It was bad enough doing this without also being paid for it.' He fished in his wallet and pulled out a big handful of notes.

'Take these.'

'Really, please, you owe me nothing.'

'But look, I've got lots.'

'No, no money.'

'I want you to have it.'

'Well, there is a charity box out there at reception, if you like.'

The nurses told me he stuffed it full of cash and left. I couldn't concentrate on the rest of the surgery and immediately we closed, I rang him at home but there was no reply.

The next morning Romsey Police arrived asking if he had been to the surgery the previous evening. The nurses and I were the last to have seen him alive. He had driven up from the clinic into some woods and put a hose pipe from the exhaust into his car window. I later had a call from his brother, who assured me that he had not at all needed to go into a home; he was invited and warmly welcomed to come and live with him, with the two cats. But he could not live without his beloved wife; he had made his decision and I hope that there had been nothing more that I could have done.

Please forgive me for ending these pages on such a sad note. It was one of the incidents that precipitated my decision to sell up there and then and return to academic life. Sometimes human behaviour was just too complex for me. I don't think I would have made a good doctor but hope I was a good vet and certainly have experienced the greatest joys in those years, and many upsets too. Difficult as it is to get into, immensely hard as the long university period proves and studded as a vet's day is with heartache as well as pleasure, it is still the best profession in the world.

I loved writing this book and thank you for reading it.

THE END

Postscript

This book originated when both my teenage daughters at different times asked me if I'd ever thought of writing an autobiography. The dear creatures bear some absurd notion that I have had a fascinating life. I got down to it but getting to the veterinary part, a strange thing happened. Recollections, names and even conversations with people I hadn't thought about for decades came flooding back. And putting it all down, that opened up more memories, anecdotes and situations, in copious volumes. I could not believe how much of it there was and for how long it had been buried.

So, I temporarily put the autobiography aside and wrote these pages instead. In including the real names of all those involved I suppose I must have been planning, when it was finished, to go through them and change them all to pseudonyms, if it were published. But then I thought, why? For one thing, false names in memoirs always strike me as contrived and phony.

And for another, they are true accounts of real people, so why not leave them as they are? I am in contact with

Postscript

almost none of them now and could not obtain their permission one way or the other, so why bother? Some of them will be no longer with us and to find the rest would be impossible. So, I offer the real names as I do the real tales; they are indivisible. And they are my tribute to those colleagues, clients and animal owners who made this writing possible.

As a rookie writer, no mainstream publisher was interested in even reading the text, so I went ahead and published it this way with the help of Paul Hawkins my typesetter, cover designer and uploader onto the Amazon platform. His help was pivotal and his website is on the copyright page.

Finally, I have a sequel in mind with fresh anecdotes and if I get down to writing it, I include here my email address (johnhsampson@orange.fr). For any colleagues or animal owners who enjoyed the book and would like to let me have some of their own vet stories, if the sequel is published and proves a success, I undertake to share the royalties with them as contributors - either attributed or anonymous. Alternatively, the money would be credited to VETLIFE, the fine charity which for many decades was known as the Veterinary Benevolent Fund, which generously helps the families of vets fallen upon hard times.

Bibliography

Goldacre, Ben, *Bad Science*. London: Fourth Estate, 2009.
Pemberton, Max, *Trust Me, I'm a (Junior) Doctor*. London: Hodder & Stoughton, 2008.

About the Author

After selling his practice in Romsey, Hampshire, John Sampson went to the University of Southampton studying for a BA in French and Spanish and then an MPhil in Linguistics. He used the long vacations to do veterinary locum work around the world which forms the basis of many of the anecdotes in the book. He now works as a translator and writer in Normandy with his French wife and teenage daughters.

Printed in Great Britain
by Amazon